10 Minute Guide to Lotus 1-2-3® Release 5 for Windows™

Peter Aitken

A Division of Macmillan Computer Publishing
201 W. 103rd Street, Indianapolis, Indiana 46290 USA

© 1994 by Que® Corporation

International Standard Book Number: 1-56761-484-1
Library of Congress Catalog Card Number: 94-70522

97 96   9 8 7 6 5

Interpretation of the printing code: the rightmost double-digit number is the year of the book's printing; the rightmost single-digit number is the number of the book's printing. For example, a printing code of 94-1 shows that the first printing of the book was in 1994.

Publisher: *Marie Butler-Knight*
Managing Editor: *Elizabeth Keaffaber*
Acquisitions Manager: *Barry Pruett*
Product Development Manager: *Faithe Wempen*
Manuscript Editor: *Audra Gable*
Cover Designer: *Dan Armstrong*
Designer: *Barbara Webster*
Indexer: *Carol Repasi*
Production: *Diana Bigham, Katy Bodenmiller, Brad Chinn, Tim Cox, Mark Enochs, Linda Koopman, Tom Loveman, Beth Rago, Joe Ramon, Carrie Roth, Greg Simsic*

Special thanks to Kelly Oliver for ensuring the technical accuracy of this book.

Screen reproductions in this book were created by means of the program Collage Plus from Inner Media, Inc., Hollis, NH.

Printed in the United States of America

Contents

Introduction, vii

1 Starting and Exiting 1-2-3 for Windows, 1

Starting 1-2-3, 1
The 1-2-3 Screen, 2
Exiting 1-2-3 for Windows, 4

2 Using 1-2-3 Menus and Dialog Boxes, 5

1-2-3 Menu Structure, 5
Making Menu Selections, 8
Dialog Boxes, 9

3 Using SmartIcons, 12

What Is a SmartIcon?, 12
Moving and Hiding the SmartIcons, 13
The Default SmartIcons, 14
Displaying Different SmartIcon Sets, 14

4 Moving Around 1-2-3 for Windows, 16

Worksheet Structure, 16
Moving Around in a Worksheet File, 18
Adding New Worksheets to a Worksheet File, 20
Navigating Between Worksheets, 21
Viewing Multiple Worksheets at Once, 22

5 Entering and Editing Data, 25

Data Types, 25
Entering Values, 27
Entering Labels, 27
Entering Dates and Times, 29
Editing Data, 30

6 Saving and Retrieving Worksheets, 33

Saving a Worksheet, 33
Opening a Worksheet File, 35
Starting a New Worksheet File, 37
Closing a Worksheet, 37

7 Working with Ranges, 39

What Is a Range?, 39
Three-Dimensional Ranges, 42
Using Range Names, 44

8 Copying, Moving, and Erasing Data, 46

Copying and Moving Data, 46
Erasing Data, 48
The Undo Command, 49

9 Inserting and Deleting Rows and Columns, 52

Inserting New Rows and Columns, 52
Deleting Rows and Columns, 54

10 Writing Formulas, 57

What Is a Formula?, 57
Entering a Formula, 58
Formula Operators and Operator Precedence, 60
Understanding Relative and Absolute Cell Addressing, 61

11 Using 1-2-3 for Windows' Built-In Formulas, 63

What Is an @Function?, 63
Using @Functions, 64
Using the @Function Selector, 67

12 Changing Number and Label Format, 69

Why Worry About Format?, 69
The Numeric Display Formats, 69
Changing the Numeric Display Format, 73
Changing Alignment, 74
Changing the Default Display
    Format and Alignment, 76

13 Changing Column Width and Row Height, 78

Changing Column Width, 78
Changing Row Height, 82

14 Using Fonts, Borders, and Styles, 85

Changing the Font, 85
Changing the Default Worksheet Font, 88
Adding Borders and Frames, 88
Using Named Styles, 90

15 Printing Your Worksheet, 93

Printing with the Default Settings, 93
Previewing a Print Job, 94
Changing Page Setup, 96

16 Creating and Printing a Chart, 102

Chart Basics, 102
Chart Types, 103
Creating a Default Chart, 105
How Default Charts Are Made, 107
Changing Chart Type, 109
Moving and Resizing a Chart, 110
Saving Charts, 111
Printing Charts, 112

17 Enhancing a Chart, 113

Chart Enhancements, 113
Adding Chart Titles and Footnotes, 113
Adding a Legend, 115
Moving Chart Titles, Footnotes, and Legends, 117

18 More Chart Enhancements, 119

Adding Axis Titles, 119
Changing Axis Scale, 121
Changing Axis Unit Titles, 122

19 Using Graphics, 124

What Are Graphics?, 124
Drawing Lines, Arcs, and Arrows, 125

Drawing Rectangles and Ellipses, 126
Creating a Text Block, 126
Modifying Graphic Objects, 128
Modifying Lines and Colors, 128
Making a Graphic
   Object Transparent, 130

20   Creating a Database, 131

Database Fundamentals, 131
Creating a Database Table, 133

21   Sorting a Database, 136

Sorting a Database, 136

22   Searching a Database, 140

Searching for Information, 140
Criteria Basics, 141
Performing a Query, 142
Finding Records, 145

A   Microsoft Windows Primer, 147

Starting Microsoft Windows, 147
Parts of a Windows Screen, 148
Using a Mouse, 149
Starting a Program, 150
Using Menus, 150
Navigating Dialog Boxes, 152
Switching Between Windows, 153
Controlling and Resizing a Window, 154

B   Table of Functions, 156

Index, 161

Introduction

Lotus 1-2-3 is one of the most popular applications programs ever, and the Microsoft Windows operating environment has taken the PC world by storm over the past few years. It was inevitable that the two would come together as Lotus 1-2-3 for Windows, which was originally introduced a couple of years ago. Shortly thereafter Release 4 came out, providing a major overhaul of the program. Now we have Release 5, with additional enhancements in power and ease of use. This great program just keeps getting better!

If you're one of the many people just starting with 1-2-3 for Windows, you're probably looking for a quick method of learning the most important features of the program. You want to get up and running quickly, and start using 1-2-3 for Windows productively. You don't have the time to sit down and read the program documentation or a 600-page book. You can however, find 10 minutes here and there in your busy schedule.

Welcome to the *10 Minute Guide to Lotus 1-2-3 for Windows*! This book is, I believe, just what you need. It teaches you the basics of 1-2-3 for Windows in a series of short lessons that can be completed in 10 minutes or less. Because each lesson is self-contained, you can start and stop as your schedule allows. This and other features of the *10 Minute Guide to Lotus 1-2-3 for Windows* make it ideal for anyone who:

- Has a limited amount of time to spend learning the program.

- Is overwhelmed by the complexity of 1-2-3 for Windows.

- Wants a clear, concise guide to the program's most important features.

- Needs to determine if 1-2-3 for Windows will meet his or her needs.

What Is the 10 Minute Guide?

The 10 Minute Guide series is a new approach to learning computer programs. Instead of trying to teach you every detail of a program, the 10 Minute Guide teaches you how to use just those features that are essential.

Each 10 Minute Guide contains more than 20 short lessons. The 10 Minute Guide teaches you about programs without relying on technical jargon—you'll find only plain English used to explain the procedures in this book. With straightforward, easy-to-follow steps and special artwork (icons) to call your attention to important tips and definitions, the 10 Minute Guide makes learning a new software program fast and easy.

Conventions Used in This Book

The following icons help you find your way around the *10 Minute Guide to Lotus 1-2-3 for Windows*:

Timesaver Tips offer shortcuts and hints for using the program more effectively.

Plain English icons identify definitions of new terms.

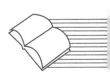

Panic Button icons appear in places where new users often run into trouble.

In addition, these specific conventions will help you find your way around the *10 Minute Guide to Lotus 1-2-3 for Windows* as easily as possible:

1. Numbered steps	Step-by-step instructions are highlighted with bold numbers in color so you can find basic 1-2-3 for Windows procedures quickly.
What you press	The keys you press and the commands you select will appear in color.
What you type	The information you type will be in bold, color computer type.
What you see on-screen	The text you see on-screen will appear in computer type.
Menu names	The names of 1-2-3 for Windows menus, options, and activities are displayed with the first letter capitalized.

Selection letters	The letters you press to pull down menus and activate menu options are printed in bold type.

The inside front cover provides instructions for installing 1-2-3 for Windows; the inside back cover shows the 1-2-3 for Windows SmartIcons, one of the program's most innovative features.

The *10 Minute Guide to Lotus 1-2-3 for Windows* contains 22 lessons. Most readers will want to work through the lessons in order. After reading the first five lessons, however, you can jump around if you need to find specific information quickly. Once you've finished this book, you may want a more detailed book on 1-2-3 for Windows. Here are some titles that I recommend:

The First Book of 1-2-3 for Windows

10 Minute Guide to Windows 3.1

Trademarks

All terms mentioned in this book that are known to be service marks are listed below. In addition, terms suspected of being trademarks or service marks have been appropriately capitalized. Que cannot attest to the accuracy of this information. Use of a term in this book should not be regarded as affecting the validity of any trademark or service mark.

Lotus is a registered trademark of Lotus Development Corporation.

Microsoft Windows is a registered trademark of Microsoft Corporation.

Starting and Exiting 1-2-3 for Windows

In this lesson, you'll learn how to start 1-2-3 for Windows and what the major parts of the 1-2-3 screen are. You'll also learn how to exit the program.

Starting 1-2-3

To start 1-2-3 for Windows, it must be installed on your system. (Refer to the inside back cover of this book for installation instructions.) Start 1-2-3 for Windows from the Windows Program Manager screen. After you have installed 1-2-3, the Program Manager screen includes a Lotus Applications window. (See Figure 1.1.)

Terminology Trouble? If Windows terms like *program group*, *icon*, and *click* scare you, turn to the Windows Primer (Appendix A) at the end of this book for help..

Start 1-2-3 for Windows by selecting the 1-2-3 icon in the Lotus Applications window. Follow these steps:

1. Open the Program Manager window, if it is not visible, by double-clicking on its icon with the mouse or by pressing Alt+Esc one or more times.

2. If necessary, open the Lotus Applications window by double-clicking on its program group icon, or by pressing Ctrl+Tab until is it highlighted and then pressing Enter.

3. Double-click on the 1-2-3 for Windows icon, or use the arrow keys to highlight the icon and then press Enter.

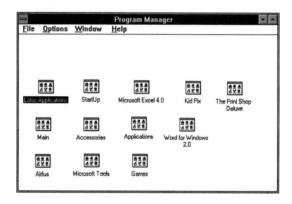

Figure 1.1   The Windows Program Manager screen.

The 1-2-3 Screen

When it starts, 1-2-3 for Windows displays its opening logo for a few seconds, and then displays the 1-2-3 screen with a blank worksheet (see Figure 1.2). You'll also see a dialog box titled Welcome to 1-2-3. You can explore this dialog box on your own later, if you wish. For now press the Esc key to close the dialog box. Figure 1.2 identifies these important components of the 1-2-3 screen:

- *Title bar*   Displays the name of the program.

- *Menu bar*   Displays 1-2-3 commands.

- *Selection indicator*　Shows the address or name of the current worksheet selection.

- *Contents box*　Used to display, enter, and edit data.

- *SmartIcons*　Let you perform common tasks by clicking with the mouse.

- *Worksheet window*　Contains the data in your worksheet.

- *Cell pointer*　A rectangle that indicates the current worksheet cell.

- *Status bar*　Displays 1-2-3 status information.

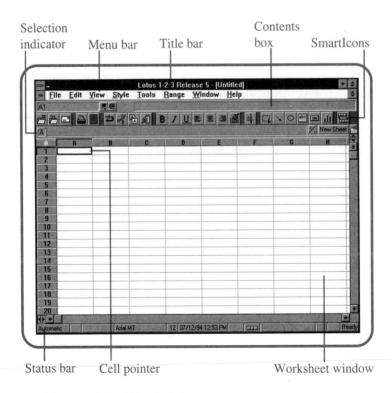

Figure 1.2　The 1-2-3 screen.

Many of the elements in the 1-2-3 for Windows screen will seem familiar to Windows users, including the title bar and menu bar. Like all Windows programs, 1-2-3 uses pull-down menus to access commands. 1-2-3 menus have a few differences from regular Windows menus, though, which you'll discover in Lesson 2.

Exiting 1-2-3 for Windows

When you're finished working with 1-2-3 for Windows, you need to exit the program in order to free up memory for other Windows applications or to turn off your computer. To exit 1-2-3 for Windows, press Alt+F4 or select File Exit. If you have any unsaved data, 1-2-3 will ask you whether the file(s) should be saved. Then 1-2-3 for Windows will disappear.

In this lesson, you learned how to start and exit the 1-2-3 for Windows program, and you learned about the important parts of the 1-2-3 screen. In the next lesson, you'll learn how to use 1-2-3 menus and dialog boxes.

Lesson 2

Using 1-2-3 Menus and Dialog Boxes

In this lesson, you'll learn how to use 1-2-3 for Windows' menus and dialog boxes.

1-2-3 Menu Structure

When working with 1-2-3 for Windows, you must use commands to instruct the program to carry out the desired tasks. Commands are often entered by means of menus. Windows users may be familiar with menu basics already, but beware—1-2-3 adds a few new menu twists.

There are four types of menus in 1-2-3 for Windows:

* The *menu bar* is displayed on the second line of the screen.

* A *pull-down menu* is associated with each command on the menu bar. When you choose a command on the menu bar, the corresponding pull-down menu is displayed, and a description of the highlighted command appears in the title bar.

- A *cascade menu* is associated with some (but not all) pull-down menu commands. A cascade menu is displayed when you choose a pull-down menu command that has an arrowhead next to it.

- A *quick menu* is displayed when you click on certain screen objects, such as a cell or a chart, with the right mouse button. A quick menu contains commands for working with the selected object.

The first three types of menus are shown in Figure 2.1. When the menu system is active, the title bar at the top of the screen displays a brief description of the currently highlighted menu command. In Figure 2.1, the Tools Draw Line command is highlighted.

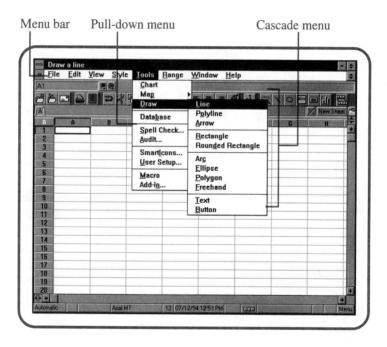

Figure 2.1 Three types of menus in 1-2-3 for Windows.

The pull-down and cascade menus use several conventions to provide additional information about the menu commands.

* A menu item is displayed in grayed text when it is not currently available.

* A keystroke combination listed after a menu command (called an accelerator key) is a way to execute the menu command directly without using the menu system.

* An ellipsis following a menu command indicates that the menu command leads to a dialog box.

* An arrowhead following a pull-down menu command indicates that the command leads to a cascade menu.

* An underlined letter in a menu command denotes the key that can be pressed to select that command when the menu is displayed.

* The movable menu pointer indicates the command that will be executed if you press Enter.

Using Accelerator Keys   You'll save time if you learn the accelerator keys for commands you use frequently.

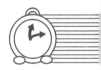

A quick menu is shown in Figure 2.2. This menu was displayed by clicking with the right mouse button on a single worksheet cell.

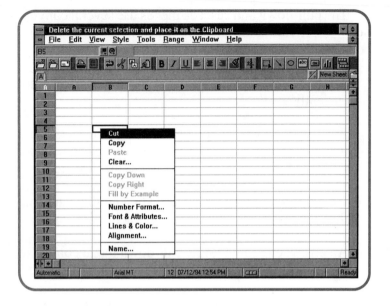

Figure 2.2 A quick menu is displayed near the screen object you clicked.

Making Menu Selections

You can select menu commands using the mouse, the keyboard, or the two used in combination. To select a command from the menu bar and display its pull-down menu:

• Using the mouse, click on the desired command.

• Using the keyboard, press Alt or F10 to activate the menu bar. Then press the letter that corresponds to the desired command (the underlined letter), or move the menu pointer to the desired command using the right and left arrow keys and press Enter.

To select a command from a pull-down or cascade menu:

* Using the mouse, click on the desired command.

* Using the keyboard, press the letter that corresponds to the desired command (the underlined letter), or move the menu pointer to the desired command using the arrow keys and press Enter.

To select a command from a quick menu, click on the desired command.

When entering menu commands, you can cancel your most recent choice by pressing Esc. To cancel an entire command sequence, click anywhere outside the menu box.

Cancelling a Command   If you enter the wrong command, cancel it by pressing Esc one or more times.

For the remainder of this book, menu command sequences will be condensed. For example, if I say select **Tools Draw Line**, it means to select Tools from the menu bar, select Draw from the pull-down menu, and then select Line from the cascade menu.

Dialog Boxes

Some commands open dialog boxes, which let you provide additional information. 1-2-3's dialog boxes are the same as those in other Windows programs. Figures 2.3 and 2.4 show a quick summary of dialog box components.

Text box 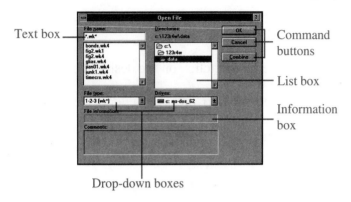 Command buttons

List box

Information box

Drop-down boxes

Figure 2.3 Components of a dialog box.

Option buttons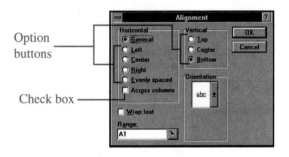

Check box

Figure 2.4 Components of a dialog box.

- A text box is used to enter and edit text information.

- A list box displays a list of items from which you can choose. If the list is too big to display at one time, a vertical scroll bar lets you scroll up and down the list. (You'll learn more about scroll bars soon.)

- A drop-down box is similar to a list box, but displays only a single item unless it is opened.

- An information box displays information about the item selected in the list box.

- Check boxes turn options on (an X is displayed) or off (no X is displayed). One or more check box options can be on at a time.

- Option buttons also turn options on or off. However, only one option button in a group can be on at a time.

- The command buttons either confirm or cancel the dialog box.

For more information on dialog boxes, see the Windows Primer (Appendix A) at the end of the book.

In this lesson, you learned how to use 1-2-3 for Windows' menus and dialog boxes. In the next lesson, you'll be introduced to SmartIcons.

Lesson 3

Using SmartIcons

In this lesson, you'll learn how to use SmartIcons and how to customize the SmartIcon set.

What Is a SmartIcon?

A SmartIcon is a small graphic symbol that is displayed on the 1-2-3 screen. Each SmartIcon is associated with an important worksheet command or task; when you click the SmartIcon, the task or command is executed immediately. Figure 3.1 shows the default SmartIcon set. 1-2-3 displays different SmartIcon sets depending on the task you are performing. (For example, there will be one set of SmartIcons available when you are entering data and a different set available when you are working on a graph.) You can control which SmartIcon set is displayed, and can customize each SmartIcon set as well. You must have a mouse to use SmartIcons.

What Does That SmartIcon Do?   To see what a SmartIcon does, point at it for a few seconds (don't click!). 1-2-3 will display a small balloon containing a description of the SmartIcon.

SmartIcons

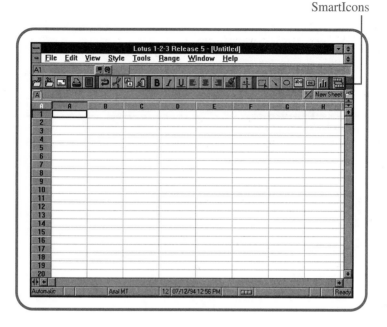

Figure 3.1 SmartIcons enable you to execute commonly needed commands by clicking.

Moving and Hiding the SmartIcons

The default SmartIcon position is near the top of the 1-2-3 screen (see Figure 3.1). You can change the position of the SmartIcons to the left, right, top, or bottom of the screen, or hide them altogether. You can choose floating SmartIcons to place them in a window that you can move to any screen location by dragging it with the mouse. You can also resize the floating SmartIcon window by grabbing one of the borders with the mouse and dragging.

To move the SmartIcons:

1. Select Tools SmartIcons.

2. In the dialog box, select the desired palette position from the Position drop-down box.

3. Select OK. The SmartIcons are displayed in the selected position.

To hide or re-display the SmartIcons:

1. Select View Set View Preferences.

2. Turn the SmartIcons check box on or off.

3. Select OK.

The Default SmartIcons

The default SmartIcon set contains those SmartIcons that you will use most frequently while entering and editing worksheet data. The inside front cover of this book shows the default SmartIcon set and gives descriptions of their functions in left-to-right order.

Displaying Different SmartIcon Sets

1-2-3 will automatically display a different SmartIcon set when you are performing certain activities, such as working on a chart. However, you can display a different set than the one shown. To display a different SmartIcon set, click the

SmartIcons button on the status bar (Figure 3.2) and then select a set from the list.

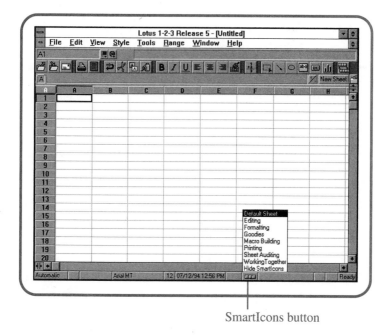

SmartIcons button

Figure 3.2   Select the SmartIcon set to display by clicking the SmartIcons button on the status bar.

In this lesson, you learned how to use SmartIcons. In the next lesson, you'll learn to move around in 1-2-3 for Windows.

Moving Around 1-2-3 for Windows

In this lesson, you'll learn the structure of a worksheet and how to move around 1-2-3 for Windows.

Worksheet Structure

1-2-3 for Windows keeps data in worksheets. A worksheet is a page that is ruled into 8,192 rows and 256 columns. The columns are identified from left to right by letters A through Z, AA through AZ, BA through BZ, and so on up to IV. The rows are numbered top to bottom, 1 through 8,192. Column letters and row numbers are shown in the worksheet frame, at the left and top edges of every worksheet window.

A 1-2-3 worksheet file is not just a single worksheet—it can contain up to 256 worksheets (like a book that contains 256 pages!). Each new worksheet file starts with a single worksheet. You can then add up to 255 more worksheets to it. Each worksheet is labeled by a tab just above the column letters. The worksheets in a worksheet file are automatically labeled A: through IV:, but you can assign your own descriptive names to them if you want.

Changing a Worksheet Name To change the name of a worksheet, double-click its tab, type in the new name, and then press Enter.

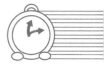

Every cell in a worksheet file has a unique position, or address. A cell address specifies the cell's worksheet, column, and row position, such as

A:B2   Worksheet A, column B, row 2

D:F21   Worksheet D, column F, row 21

Every worksheet file has a single current cell, indicated by the cell pointer. The cell pointer is movable (you'll see how soon), and the address of the current cell is displayed in the selection indicator. In addition, the worksheet frame highlights the letter and number of the current cell. Figure 3.1 illustrates cell addresses; cell B5 is current in the figure.

Tab indicates which worksheet is active.   Column B

Figure 4.1 Cell addresses in a worksheet file.

17

Moving Around in a Worksheet File

A worksheet usually contains more information than can be viewed at once in the worksheet window. You can scroll the contents of a worksheet to bring different regions into view. You can use either the keyboard or the mouse to scroll. To scroll with the mouse you use the scroll bars. The components of a scroll bar are shown in Figure 4.2.

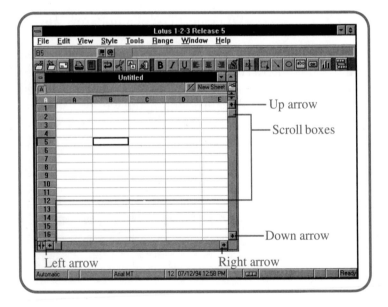

Figure 4.2 The components of a scroll bar.

Table 4.1 shows some techniques for using the scroll bar.

Table 4.1   Using scroll bars with the mouse.

To scroll . . .	Do this . . .
Up or down one row	Click the up or down arrow on the vertical scroll bar.
Left or right one column	Click the left or right arrow on the horizontal scroll bar.
Up or down one screen	Click the vertical scroll bar between the up or down arrow and the scroll box.
Left or right one screen	Click the horizontal scroll bar between the left or right arrow and the scroll box.
To the top or bottom row	Drag the scroll box to the top or bottom of the vertical scroll bar.
To the leftmost or rightmost column	Drag the scroll box to the left or right end of the horizontal scroll bar.
To a variable position	Drag the vertical or horizontal scroll box to the desired position.

When you scroll using the scroll bars, the cell pointer does not move. You can use the mouse to move the cell pointer large distances by scrolling to bring the desired area into view, and then clicking the desired cell.

You can also use the keyboard to scroll to different regions of the worksheet. Unlike with mouse scrolling, when you scroll using the keyboard, the cell pointer moves with you so that it always remains in view. Table 4.2 shows keyboard scrolling techniques.

Table 4.2 Using scroll bars with the keyboard.

To move the cell pointer	Press
Up or down one row	↑ or ↓
Left or right one column	← or →
Up or down one screen	PgUp or PgDn
Right one screen	Ctrl+→ or Tab
Left one screen	Ctrl+← or Shift+Tab
To cell A1	Home
To any cell	F5 (the GoTo key), then type the cell address and then press Enter.

The End key can be used along with the navigation keys for rapid movement of the cell pointer. Press End followed by an arrow key, and the pointer moves in the indicated direction until it reaches the first boundary between an empty cell and a non-empty cell. If the row or column is empty, the pointer moves to the edge of the worksheet. Press End followed by Home to move to the lower right corner of the worksheet region that contains data.

Moving Quickly to Cell A1 To move the cell pointer to the top of the worksheet (cell A1), press Home.

Adding New Worksheets to a Worksheet File

A worksheet file originally contains only a single worksheet, worksheet A. For many applications, a single worksheet is all you'll need. To use additional worksheets, you must add them to the file. To insert an additional worksheet into a worksheet file:

1. Select Edit Insert.

2. In the dialog box, select the Sheet option button.

3. Select Before or After.

4. Select OK.

After these steps, your worksheet file will contain two worksheets, A and B.

Adding More Than One Worksheet?   Use the Quantity option in the dialog box to insert more than one new worksheet at a time.

Get a New Worksheet Fast!   To quickly insert a single new worksheet, click the New Sheet button.

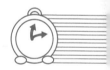

Navigating Between Worksheets

When your worksheet file contains more than one worksheet, you can move the cell pointer between worksheets using the keyboard in the following manner:

Press	To move the cell pointer
Ctrl+PgUp	To the next worksheet (from A: to B:, for example).
Ctrl+PgDn	To the previous worksheet (from B: to A:, for example).

Press	To move the cell pointer
Ctrl+Home	To cell A1 in worksheet A:.
End Ctrl+Home	To the cell in the lower right corner of the last worksheet in the file's data-containing area.
End Ctrl+PgUp	Backward through worksheets (staying in the same row and column) to the first boundary between an empty and non-empty cell.
End Ctrl+PgDn	Forward through worksheets (staying in the same row and column) to the first boundary between an empty and non-empty cell.

Moving Between Worksheets with the Mouse
To move to another worksheet using the mouse, click on the worksheet's tab.

Viewing Multiple Worksheets at Once

Even if your worksheet file contains multiple worksheets, a worksheet window normally displays only one of them at a time. This is the *current* worksheet, the one containing the cell pointer. You can display another worksheet by moving the cell pointer into it (as was explained above). You can also display up to three worksheets in a single window by selecting Perspective view. Figure 4.3 shows a maximized worksheet window displaying three worksheets in Perspective view. To display multiple worksheets in Perspective view:

1. Select View Split.

2. In the dialog box select Perspective and then select OK.

3. To cancel Perspective view and return to a single worksheet display, select View Clear Split.

Synchronizing Your Worksheets   If you select the Synchronized Scrolling option in the Split dialog box, the three worksheets displayed in Perspective view will scroll together so that the same rows and columns are always visible in all three worksheets.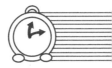

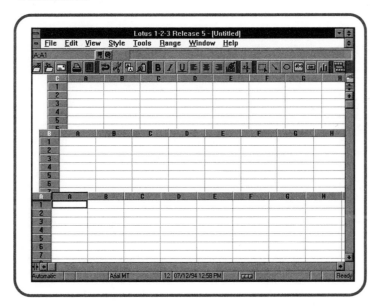

Figure 4.3   Perspective view enables you to view three worksheets in a single window.

 **Keeping It in Perspective** In Perspective view, press F6 to move the cell pointer to another worksheet.

In this lesson, you learned about worksheet structure, cell addresses, and how to move around in 1-2-3 for Windows. The next lesson shows you how to enter and edit worksheet data.

Lesson 5

Entering and Editing Data

In this lesson, you'll learn about 1-2-3 for Windows data types, and how to enter and edit worksheet data.

Data Types

A worksheet cell can hold either a *value* or a *label*. (A third type of data that a cell can contain, formulas, is discussed in Lesson 10.) A value is a number; a label is any sequence of characters that can't be used for calculations (for instance, a name). When you enter data into a worksheet cell, 1-2-3 can tell whether the entry is a value or a label by the characters you type. The following characters indicate a value:

- Any number (0–9)

- + – (.

- Any currency symbol (such as $)

All other characters signal a label entry (except for certain formula characters, which you'll learn about later). When you begin entering data, the 1-2-3 mode indicator at the right end of the status bar shows Value or Label, depending on the data type being entered.

25

When you start typing an entry, characters you enter appear in the current cell and also in the contents box. Figure 5.1 shows how the worksheet would appear if you moved the cell pointer to cell B3 and typed 123 (before you confirmed the entry).

Cancel box   Confirm box

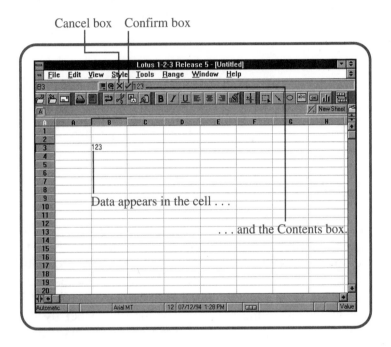

Figure 5.1   As you enter data, it appears in the cell and in the contents box.

When you start typing a data entry, 1-2-3 displays the Confirm box (a check mark) and the Cancel box (an X) next to the contents box (see Figure 5.1). You can click on these boxes to either confirm or cancel an entry. When you confirm your entry, 1-2-3 enters it in the current worksheet cell. If other data already exists in the cell, the old data is replaced by the new entry.

Before confirming an entry, you can edit or cancel it. To cancel a data entry, click the Cancel box or press Esc. If you cancel an entry, the cell is not changed. To edit a data entry, press Backspace to erase the mistake, and then type replacement characters. To edit an entry after you have confirmed it, follow the instructions given later in this chapter.

Entering Values

Values are entered from the keyboard. To enter a value in a worksheet cell follow these steps:

1. Move the cell pointer to the desired cell.

2. Type the desired value.

3. Confirm the entry by pressing Enter, by moving the cell pointer to another cell, or by clicking the Confirm box (see Figure 5.1).

Entering Labels

1-2-3 for Windows stores labels with a *label prefix character* at the beginning. The label prefix character identifies the entry as a label and controls how it is displayed in the cell, as shown in Figure 5.2. The label prefix character is not displayed in the worksheet, but is shown in the contents box when the cell pointer is on a label cell. There are three label prefix characters that determine how the label is displayed in the cell:

'	Left aligned in the cell
"	Right aligned in the cell
^	Centered in the cell

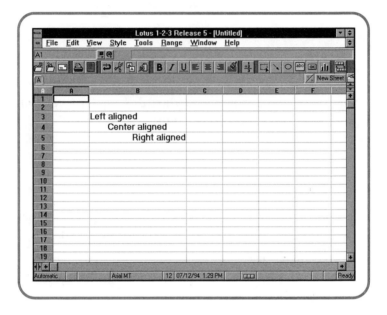

Figure 5.2 The label prefix character controls how a label is aligned in the cell.

1-2-3 automatically inserts the label prefix character when you start typing a label entry. The default label prefix is left aligned ('). If you enter a label that starts with a number but contains non-numeric characters (for example, a street address such as 5 Main St.), 1-2-3 will also automatically add the label prefix character. Therefore, you must enter the label prefix character yourself to enter a label that contains only numbers, or that starts with one of these characters:

+ = − < $ (# @ / \

A label can be up to 512 characters long, which means that you can enter a label that is wider than the cell. If the cells to the immediate right are empty, 1-2-3 will display the entire label, overlapping the empty cells to the right. If the cells to the right are occupied, 1-2-3 will display only part of the label. The entire label is, however, stored in the worksheet and will be displayed in the contents box when the cell pointer is on that cell.

Entering Dates and Times

1-2-3 for Windows stores dates and times as special serial numbers.

Date   A value between 1 and 73,050 representing the number of days since December 31, 1899.

Time   A decimal fraction between 0.0 and 0.9999884 representing the 24-hour day, 12:00AM to 12:59:59PM.

Here are examples of date and time serial numbers:

Serial number	Date or time
1	January 1, 1900
73050	December 31, 2099
32978	April 15, 1990
0.0	12:00:00 AM
0.5	12:00:00 noon

To enter a date or time, you enter it directly in a cell in one of the following formats:

Day-month-year	20-Jul-93
Day-month	20-Jul
Long international	7/20/93
Long AM/PM	11:30:45 PM
Short AM/PM	11:30 PM
Long 24-hour	23:30:45
Short 24-hour	23:30

If you use these formats, 1-2-3 for Windows will automatically recognize the entry as a date or time and convert it to the corresponding serial number. 1-2-3 also sets the cell format to display the date or time the way you specify, in a readable format, even though the value stored in the cell is actually a value (the serial number). When the cell pointer is on a cell that contains a date or time, the contents box displays the serial number. 1-2-3 offers a variety of different display formats for dates and times; these are covered in Lesson 12.

Editing Data

You can delete, replace, or edit existing worksheet data. First, move the cell pointer to the cell. To delete the data, press Del. To replace the data, enter the new data as described above. To edit the data in the cell, follow these steps:

1. Double-click the cell or press F2. The insertion point, a blinking vertical line, appears at the end of the cell's data.

2. Press ←or →to move the insertion point one character at a time. Press the Home or End key to move the insertion point to the beginning or end of the data.

   Press Del to delete the character to the right of the insertion point, or press Backspace to delete the character to the left of the insertion point.

   Enter new characters as needed.

3. When you are finished, press Enter or click on the Confirm box.

You can also edit data in the contents box. This is convenient for editing long labels. Here are the steps to follow:

1. Move the cell pointer to the cell you want to edit.

2. Click in the contents box. The insertion point appears where you clicked.

3. Move the insertion point and delete and enter characters as described above.

4. When you are finished, press Enter or click on the Confirm box.

Oops! If you make a mistake while editing a cell, click the Cancel box to restore the cell's original contents.

In this lesson, you learned that 1-2-3 for Windows' cells can contain values or labels. You also learned how to enter data into a worksheet, and how to edit existing data. The next lesson shows you how to save and retrieve files.

Lesson 6

Saving and Retrieving Worksheets

In this lesson, you'll learn how to save your worksheets on disk and retrieve them later.

Saving a Worksheet

As you work in 1-2-3 for Windows, your worksheet data is kept in the computer's random-access memory, or RAM. RAM is temporary storage that is erased each time the system is turned off. To save your work permanently, you must save it to a file on a disk (either a diskette or a fixed disk). Each worksheet file is saved in a separate file on the disk.

To save a worksheet file under its existing name, use the File Save command. By existing name, I mean the name displayed in the worksheet's title bar. The only exception to this is when the title bar displays Untitled, as the default worksheet does when you first start 1-2-3 for Windows. In this case, the File Save command automatically assigns a default file name of the form FILE*nnnn*.WK4, where *nnnn* is a sequential number.

You should avoid using the default file names. It's much better to assign your own names that describe the files contents: SALES93, EXPENSES, MEDICAL, TAXES, and so on. 1-2-3 for Windows automatically adds the extension .WK4 to all file names.

To save an untitled worksheet file and assign it a name, follow these steps.

1. Select File Save. Because the file has not yet been named, 1-2-3 displays the File Save As dialog box (shown in Figure 6.1).

2. In the dialog box, select the File name text box. You can edit the default name that is displayed there, or enter a new name. A file name consists of 1–8 characters.

3. If desired, use the Directories list box and the Drives drop-down box to select a different drive and/or directory.

4. Select OK. The file is saved to disk under the name you entered. The file's new name is now displayed in the title bar.

Once a file has been assigned a name, you can save it quickly with the File Save command. When you select File Save, the file is saved to disk under the name in its title bar (except for untitled worksheets, as just described). If a file with the same name already exists, it is replaced with the new version.

 Quick Save   To save a file, click the File Save SmartIcon.

File name
text box
(enter a
name for
the file).

Select
the type
of file to
save.

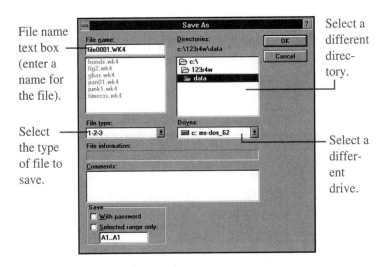

Select a
different
direc-
tory.

Select a
differ-
ent
drive.

Figure 6.1 The Save As dialog box.

Quick Help Whenever a dialog box is displayed, you can click the question mark icon in the upper right corner to view relevant help information.

Opening a Worksheet File

You can open any worksheet file that has previously been saved to disk. When you open a worksheet file, 1-2-3 opens a new window in the work area and displays the file in it. The worksheet title will remain the same unless you change it with the **File Save As** command.

To open an existing worksheet file, use the **File Open** command. In addition to WK4 files, you can open worksheet files created with Lotus 1-2-3 version 1.1 (WKS extension), version 2.x (WK1 extension), version 3.x and version 1.x for Windows (WK3 extension), Microsoft Excel (XLS extension), and Lotus Symphony (WR1 and WRK extensions). To open a worksheet file:

1. Select File Open or click the Open File SmartIcon. The Open File dialog box is displayed (Figure 6.2). The File name text box contains the name of the current disk, the current path, and the file name template (by default *.WK*). The files list box contains a list of all files that match the template.

2. If necessary, use the Directories list box and the Drives drop-down box to select another drive and/or directory.

3. If you want to list files with a different extension, open the File type drop-down box and select the desired type.

4. Select the desired file name from the files list box.

5. Select OK. 1-2-3 opens the file and displays it in a new window.

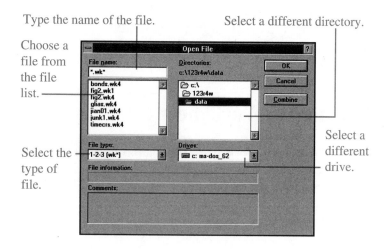

Type the name of the file.

Select a different directory.

Choose a file from the file list.

Select the type of file.

Select a different drive.

Figure 6.2 The Open File dialog box.

 Opening a Worksheet To open a worksheet file, click the Open File SmartIcon.

Combining Worksheets   The Combine button in the Open File dialog box lets you open the worksheet into an existing one. You may need this feature later as you create more advanced worksheets.

Starting a New Worksheet File

When 1-2-3 starts, it opens a new worksheet file for you. To open an additional new worksheet file, use the **File New** command. When you execute **File New**, 1-2-3 for Windows opens an empty worksheet window and assigns it a default name of the form FILE*nnnn*.WK4, as described previously. After entering data in the new worksheet, you can save it under a descriptive name using the **File Save** command.

 A New Worksheet   To start a new worksheet file, click on the New File SmartIcon.

Closing a Worksheet

When you're done working on a particular worksheet file, you can close it to remove it from the work area. To close a file, select File Close. If the file has been modified since the last time you saved it, 1-2-3 will display a prompt asking you whether the file should be saved before closing. Unless you want to discard your most recent changes to the file, select Yes. The worksheet's window will be erased from the screen. The worksheet file will remain on disk, of course, and you can open it later when you need to work on it again.

In this lesson, you learned how to save and retrieve worksheet files, how to open a new file, and how to close a file. In the next lesson, you'll learn how to work with ranges.

Lesson 7

Working with Ranges

In this lesson, you'll learn how to specify worksheet ranges and assign names to them.

What Is a Range?

Many 1-2-3 for Windows commands affect the data in worksheet cells. For example, you can erase data, copy data, or move data to another location. Before you execute a command that affects worksheet cells, you must tell 1-2-3 which cells to operate on. You do this by defining the *current selection*, the cell or cells that your next command will affect. Unless you specify otherwise, the current selection is the single cell that the cell pointer is on.

Often, however, you will work with multi-cell selections, or *ranges*. A range is a rectangular region of cells that is defined by the cells at its upper left and lower right corners. For example, B3..C14 is a range containing cells B3, C3, B4, C4, and so on up to B14 and C14. Two periods (..) mean "through," as in "cells B3 through C14." A range can be any size from a single cell to an entire worksheet.

Range A rectangular block of one or more cells, which can include anywhere from one cell to the entire worksheet.

With most 1-2-3 for Windows commands, you can specify the range to be affected either before or after selecting the command. This book uses the method of specifying a range before the command is entered. When you select a range before choosing a command, the range remains selected after the command is executed. This is useful when you need to use several commands on the same worksheet range. If you do not select a range before choosing a command that requires a range, you will be required to specify the range in the command's dialog box. See your 1-2-3 for Windows documentation for information on how to do this.

To specify a range with the mouse:

1. Move the mouse pointer to the upper left corner of the range.

2. Press and hold the left mouse button.

3. Drag the mouse pointer to the lower right corner of the range. As you drag, a highlighted rectangle expands to cover the range.

4. Release the mouse button.

To specify a range with the keyboard:

1. Use the navigation keys to move the cell pointer to one corner of the range.

2. Press F4.

3. Use the navigation keys to move the cell pointer to the diagonally opposite corner of the range. As you move the pointer, a highlighted rectangle expands to cover the range.

4. Press Enter.

Timesaver Tip   You can also press and hold the Shift key while using the navigation keys to select a range.

When you have defined a multi-cell current selection, it is highlighted. For example, in Figure 7.1 the current selection is B2..D8.

Click here to select the entire worksheet as a range.

Click on a column letter to select an entire column.

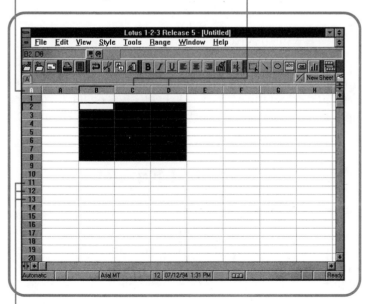

Click on a row number to select an entire row.

Figure 7.1   The current selection in the active window is highlighted.

41

If you highlight a range and then change your mind, you can cancel the selection by pressing Esc or clicking the left mouse button on any cell. After highlighting a range, you will often select a command that operates on the range. When you do this, the command's dialog box will automatically contain the range address in its **R**ange text box. You can, if you wish, edit the text box to specify a different range.

You can select an entire single column or row by clicking its letter or number. (There is no keyboard method for selecting entire columns or rows.) To select a range of columns or rows:

1. Point at the letter or number of the first column or row.

2. Press the mouse button and drag to the last column or row.

3. Release the button.

If you want to select more than one column or row, hold down the Ctrl key while you click on the column letters or rows. To select the entire worksheet, click on the box in the upper left corner of the worksheet, as shown in Figure 7.1.

Three-Dimensional Ranges

The ranges described so far have been two-dimensional, being contained entirely in a single worksheet. A three-dimensional, or 3-D, range spans two or more worksheets in a worksheet file. A 3-D range contains the same rows and columns in each worksheet. For example, a 3-D range could contain cells B2, B3, C2, and C3 in worksheets A, B, and C. This range would be indicated by the address A:B2..C:C3.

This range is highlighted in Perspective view in Figure 7.2. You do not have to be in Perspective view to specify a 3-D range.

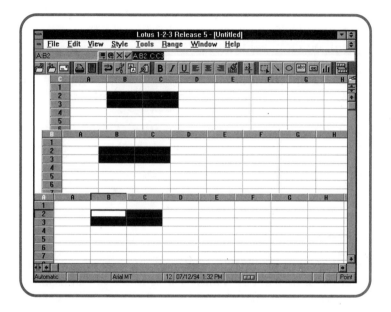

Figure 7.2   The 3-D range A:B2..C:C3 is highlighted.

You can specify a 3-D range anywhere a range is required, either before or after entering a command. You highlight a 3-D range with the keyboard or mouse. To specify a 3-D range with the mouse:

1. Move the cell pointer to the first worksheet that will be included in the range.

2. Point at the first cell and drag to highlight the desired row and column range in the worksheet.

3. Press and hold the Shift key, and then click the tab of the last worksheet to be included in the range.

To specify a 3-D range with the keyboard:

1. Move the cell pointer to the first or last worksheet that will be included in the range.

2. Using the techniques already described, highlight the desired row and column range in the worksheet.

3. Hold down the Shift key, press Ctrl+PgUp or Ctrl+PgDn to expand the range to other worksheets, and then press Enter.

Using Range Names

You'll sometimes define and use a range only once. Other ranges will be used over and over again. You can assign a name to a range, and then refer to the range by its name rather than by its address. Range names that you have assigned are saved with each worksheet file. To assign a name to a range:

1. Specify (highlight) the range to be named.

2. Select Range Name. The Name dialog box is displayed, as shown in Figure 7.3. Existing range names, if any, are displayed in the Existing named ranges list box.

3. Type the desired range name into the Name text box. A range name can be up to 15 characters long.

4. Select OK to assign the name to the range and close the dialog box.

Figure 7.3 The Name dialog box.

Displaying the Name Dialog Box To quickly display the Name dialog box, highlight a range, click it with the right mouse button, and select Name... from the quick menu.

For example, let's say you assigned the name SALES91 to the range A:A2..A:A20. You could then use the name SALES91 whenever you wanted to refer to that range. If you select a command that operates on a range and enter SALES91 in the dialog box's Range text box, the effect is the same as if you had highlighted the range A:A2..A:A20 before selecting the command. You also can use range names in 1-2-3 formulas, which are covered in Lessons 11 and 12.

This lesson showed you how to define and name ranges in your worksheets. In the next lesson, you'll learn how to copy, move, and erase worksheet data.

Lesson 8

Copying, Moving, and Erasing Data

In this lesson, you'll learn how to copy, move, and erase worksheet data and how to use the Undo feature.

Copying and Moving Data

When you copy data, the data is duplicated and will be present in both the original and the new location, as shown in Figure 8.1. You can copy data by dragging it with the mouse or by using the Clipboard (a temporary storage location maintained by Windows).

Clipboard A temporary storage location for data that you are copying or moving.

To copy data by dragging, follow these steps:

1. Highlight the range containing the data you want to copy.

2. Point at the edge of the range so the mouse pointer changes to a hand.

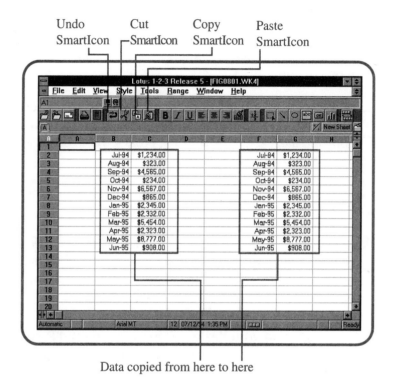

Undo SmartIcon   Cut SmartIcon   Copy SmartIcon   Paste SmartIcon

Data copied from here to here

Figure 8.1 After a copy operation, the data exists in both the old and new locations.

3. To copy the data, press and hold the Ctrl key. To move the data, do not press any key.

4. Press the mouse button and drag to the new location.

5. When the outline is positioned where you want to move or copy the data, release the mouse button. Any existing data in these cells is overwritten by the new data.

To move or copy data using the Clipboard:

1. Highlight the range containing the data you want to move or copy.

2. To delete the data and place it on the Clipboard, select Edit Cut, press Ctrl+X, or click the Cut SmartIcon. To copy the data, select Edit Copy, press Ctrl+C, or click the Copy SmartIcon.

3. Move the cell pointer to the upper left corner of the range where you want the data moved to.

4. Select Edit Paste, press Ctrl+V, or click the Paste SmartIcon to paste the data from the Clipboard into the worksheet. Any data already in these cells is overwritten by the moved data.

 **Copy, Cut, and Paste**   The Copy, Cut, and Paste commands are also available on the quick menu, which is displayed when you click on a cell or range with the right mouse button.

Erasing Data

You can erase the cell contents (data) and/or the styles from a range of cells. Styles control how data is displayed (such as font and border options). You'll learn more about styles in Lesson 14. When you erase cells you have three options:

• *Cell contents only*   The data is erased but the cells retain any special styles you have assigned. Any new data entered into the cells will be displayed with the old style.

- *Styles only* Data will remain in the cells but it will revert to the default style.

- *Both* The data is erased and the cells revert to the default style.

  To erase cell contents and/or styles:

1. Specify the range to be erased.

2. Select Edit Clear.

3. In the dialog box, select Cell contents only, Styles only, or Both.

4. Click OK.

Fast Delete To quickly delete cell contents only, press Del.

The Undo Command

The Undo command is available only when it is enabled. When you first install 1-2-3, Undo is enabled (turned on) by default. To disable Undo, which speeds up certain worksheet operations, or to reenable it when it's turned off:

1. Select Tools User Setup.

2. In the dialog box, click the Undo check box.

3. Click OK.

49

Recovering Deleted Data You can use the Edit Undo command or the Undo SmartIcon (see Figure 8.1) to recover data that you have accidentally erased.

If you mistakenly erase some valuable data, the Edit Undo command can usually save you. Generally speaking, you can undo any action or command that changes worksheet data or settings. Many 1-2-3 commands or actions can be undone with this command. Here are some examples:

- Deleting data

- Changing a cell entry

- Moving or copying data

- Changing a cell's style

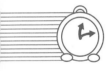

Using Undo Undo will work only if used immediately after the worksheet action you want to reverse.

Here are some things that cannot be undone:

- Changes to disk files

- A previous use of Undo

- Formula recalculation

To undo your latest action, select Edit Undo, press Ctrl+Z, or click the Undo SmartIcon.

In this lesson, you learned how to copy, move, and erase worksheet data, and how to use the Undo feature. The next lesson shows you how to insert and delete entire rows and columns.

Inserting and Deleting Rows and Columns

In this lesson, you'll learn how to insert and delete entire rows and columns in your worksheet.

Inserting New Rows and Columns

You can insert one or more new blank rows or columns in your worksheet. When you insert a row, existing data moves down one row to make room for the new row. When you insert a column, existing data moves one column to the right to make room for the new column. For example, if you position the cell pointer in column C and insert a new column, the worksheet will then contain a new, empty column C; the original column C will now be D; the original D will be E, and so on (see Figures 9.1 and 9.2).

To insert a new row or column in a worksheet.

1. Move the cell pointer to any cell in the row or column where you want the new one inserted. For example, to insert a new column between the current columns A and B, put the pointer in any cell in column B.

2. Select Edit Insert or press Ctrl++ (the + on the numeric keypad). The Insert dialog box is displayed.

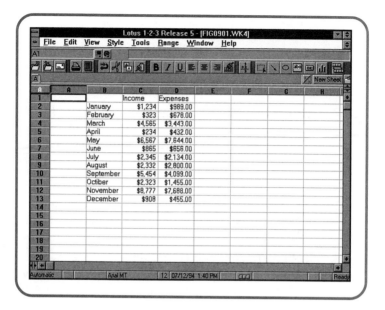

Figure 9.1 The original worksheet.

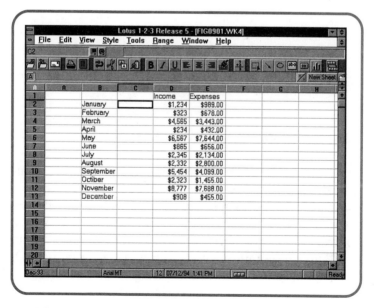

Figure 9.2 The worksheet after inserting a new column C.

3. In the dialog box, select **Row** or Column.

4. Select OK. The new row or column is inserted in the worksheet.

A Quick Insertion   To quickly insert a single new column or row, click the column letter or row number with the right mouse button. Then select Insert from the quick menu.

To insert two or more rows or columns at once, start by selecting a range that spans the desired number of columns. For example, to insert three new rows between row 2 and row 3, select any range of cells that spans rows 2, 3, and 4 (for example A2..A4). Then select Edit Insert, select **Row**, and select OK. The original rows below 1 will be moved down three rows, and the three new rows will be inserted in rows 2, 3, and 4.

Automatic Update   When you insert or delete rows or columns from your worksheet, 1-2-3 automatically adjusts cell references in formulas.

Deleting Rows and Columns

You can delete entire rows and columns from your worksheet. When you do so, the data in the deleted area is gone, and rows below the deleted row move up, or columns to the right of the deleted column move left, to fill the space. For example, if you delete column C, the original column D will now be column C, column E will now be column D, and so on (see Figures 9.2 and 9.3).

To delete one or more columns or rows:

1. Highlight a range that includes at least one cell in each row or column to be deleted.

2. Select **Edit Delete** or press **Ctrl+−** (the − on the numeric keypad).

3. In the dialog box, select **R**ow or **C**olumn.

4. Select **OK**. The specified rows or columns are deleted.

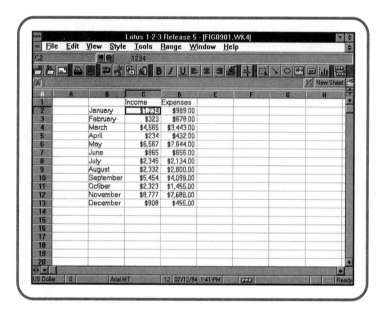

Figure 9.3   The same worksheet after deleting column C.

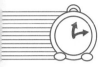

Selecting Rows and Columns To select an entire row or column and display a quick menu, click the row number or column letter with the right mouse button. To delete the selected row or column, select Delete from the quick menu.

Undoing a Row or Column Deletion If you make a mistake and delete the wrong rows or columns, you can get them back with Edit Undo (if you have not made any other changes since).

In this lesson, you learned how to insert and delete worksheet columns and rows. The next lesson shows you how to use formulas in your worksheets.

Lesson 10
Writing Formulas

In this lesson, you'll learn how to use formulas in your worksheets.

What Is a Formula?

You have learned that a worksheet cell can contain either a value or a label. A cell can also contain a formula. This is one of 1-2-3 for Windows' most powerful features. A formula is a mathematical equation that performs a calculation based on values in a worksheet. Using formulas, you can perform calculations on the numbers in your worksheet, doing such things as:

- Summing groups of values

- Calculating averages

- Performing financial analyses

A formula can contain values and can also refer to values in other worksheet cells. Whenever data in the worksheet changes, formulas are automatically recalculated, keeping the worksheet up-to-date. A cell that contains a formula displays the result of the formula, not the formula itself. However, the contents box displays the formula when the cell pointer is on the cell. Table 10.1 shows some simple formulas.

Table 10.1   Example 1-2-3 for Windows formulas.

If you enter:	The cell displays:
20/4	5 (20 divided by 4).
+B3	The contents of cell B3.
+B1+B2+B3	The sum of the values in cells B1, B2, and B3.
+Total	The contents of the cell that has been assigned the range name Total.
+<<SALES91>>A10	The value in cell A10 in the worksheet file SALES91.WK4.

Looking at these examples, note that in order to refer to the contents of another worksheet cell, a formula must include either the cell's address or its assigned range name.

Entering a Formula

You enter a formula into a cell like any other entry. A formula must begin with a number, a left parenthesis, a cell reference preceded by a plus or minus sign, or the name of an @function. (These are 1-2-3 for Windows' built-in formulas, discussed in the next lesson.) In Figure 10.1, cell B7 contains the formula +B2+B3+B4+B5+B6, calculating the sum of the values in cells B2..B6. The worksheet displays the formula result, while the contents box displays the formula (when the cell pointer is on cell B7).

The contents box displays the formula itself.

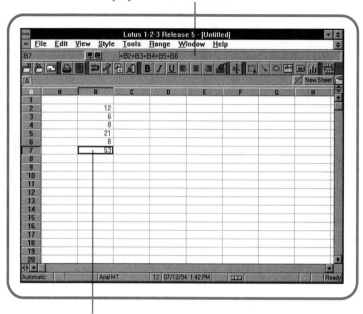

The worksheet displays the result of the formula.

Figure 10.1   The worksheet displays the result of a formula, but the contents box displays the formula itself.

ERR and Errors   If 1-2-3 cannot evaluate a formula, it displays ERR in the cell. When this happens, check the formula for errors. Common errors include leaving out a closing parenthesis or accidentally inserting a comma.

The 1-2-3 for Windows default is to display formula results in worksheet cells. When developing a complex worksheet, it is sometimes useful to have the formulas themselves displayed in the worksheet. You can do this by applying the Text format to cells. You'll learn how to do this in Lesson 12.

Editing a Formula

You can edit a formula the same way you edit any other cell entry: double-click the cell, or move the cell pointer to the cell and press F2. Details of the editing procedure were presented in Lesson 5.

Formula Operators and Operator Precedence

An *operator* is a symbol that instructs 1-2-3 to perform a certain operation in a formula. 1-2-3's operators have a precedence that determines the order in which they are performed. 1-2-3 can use the five standard mathematical operators to perform numeric calculations in formulas:

- \+   addition

- –   subtraction

- *   multiplication

- /   division

- ^   exponentiation

When a numeric formula contains more than one operator, 1-2-3 performs the operations in a particular order, or precedence. Operators with lower precedence numbers are performed first. The precedence of operators is:

Precedence	Operator(s)
1	^
2	* /
3	+ –

Operators with the same precedence are performed in left-to-right order. You can use parentheses to modify the order in which calculations are performed. Operations enclosed within parentheses are always performed first. Here are two examples:

Formula	Result
+4+2*5	14 (The * is performed first, resulting in 10; then the 4 is added.)
(4+2)*5	30 (The parentheses force the + to be performed first, resulting in 6. The 6 is then multiplied by 5.)

Understanding Relative and Absolute Cell Addressing

To use formulas effectively, you must understand the distinction between relative and absolute cell references. By default, cell addresses are *relative*. A relative cell address does not refer to a fixed worksheet location, but to a location that is relative to the cell containing the formula.

An example will make this clearer. In cell A2, enter the formula +A1. Because +A1 is a relative cell reference, the formula's meaning is "the value in the cell immediately above this cell." If you use the Copy command to copy the formula to another cell in the same worksheet, it retains its relative meaning. If, for example, you copy it to cell D8, the formula is changed to +D7, retaining its original meaning (the value in the cell immediately above this cell). Relative cell addresses are appropriate for many 1-2-3 formulas.

At times, however, you want a cell reference in a formula to refer to a specific cell or range, no matter where the formula is copied to. In this case you use an absolute reference. An absolute cell reference is denoted by a dollar sign ($) before both the column letter and row number in the address (for example, $A$1). If you enter the formula +$A$1 in cell A2 then copy it to cell D8, the copied formula will still read +$A$1.

You can enter absolute references by simply including the $ in the appropriate places as you type or edit the formula. You can also use the F4 (Abs) key to have 1-2-3 automatically put in the dollar signs for you. When you enter a formula, type the cell or range address and then stop. Press F4 to add the dollar signs, and then continue entering the formula. You can use F4 to change a cell reference while editing a formula as well.

Using Absolute References   Before copying or moving cells that contain formulas, examine the formulas to see if absolute cell references are needed.

In this lesson, you learned how to use formulas in your worksheets to perform calculations. The next lesson covers 1-2-3 for Windows' built-in formulas.

Lesson 11
Using 1-2-3 for Windows' Built-In Formulas

In this lesson you'll be introduced to 1-2-3 for Windows' built-in formulas, the @functions.

What Is an @Function?

The 1-2-3 for Windows program includes an array of built-in formulas that are called @functions ("at" functions). You can use @functions in formulas in your worksheets, either alone or as part of complex calculations. Some @functions provide a quick way to perform commonly needed calculations, such as summing a group of numbers. Other @functions let you do complex calculations, such as calculating depreciation, without you having to write the formulas yourself.

1-2-3 for Windows' @functions fall into ten categories:

- *Calendar* @functions manipulate date and time serial numbers.

- *Database* @functions perform calculations on values in database tables. (You'll learn about database tables in Lesson 20.)

- *Engineering* @functions perform engineering and advanced mathematical calculations.

- *Financial* @functions perform financial calculations, such as loan payments and annuities.

- *Information* @functions return information about cells, ranges, the operating system, and some 1-2-3 tools.

- *Logical* @functions determine whether certain conditions in the worksheet are true or false.

- *Lookup* @functions find the contents of a cell.

- *Mathematical* @functions perform mathematical calculations on values, such as calculating sums and averages.

- *Statistical* @functions perform calculations on lists of values, such as standard deviation and variance.

- *Text* @functions provide information about text in cells and perform other operations on labels.

1-2-3 for Windows has over 300 @functions. Obviously, we cannot cover them all in a 10 minute lesson! This section shows you the basics of using @functions. The Table of Functions (Appendix B) lists and describes some of the more frequently used @functions. You can also refer to the 1-2-3 for Windows documentation and the Help system for details on specific functions.

Using @Functions

An @function can be placed by itself in a cell, or it can be part of a formula. For example, to display the sum of the values in the range B1..B10, you would enter:

```
@sum(B1..B10)
```

If you wanted to display 10% of the sum of B1..B10, you would enter:

```
+0.1*@sum(B1..B10)
```

Each @function consists of the function name followed in most cases by parentheses. The function name always begins with the @ symbol. The parentheses enclose a list of one or more *arguments*. The arguments are the values or cell addresses that the function uses in its calculations. A function's arguments can be values, cell addresses, range names, or even another @function. Table 11.1 lists some example @functions:

Table 11.1 Sample @functions and their results.

@Function	Result
@sum(DATA)	The sum of all values in the range named DATA.
@pmt(5000, 0.10/12, 36)	The monthly payment on a $5000, 36-month loan at 10% annual interest.
@min(A:A1..A:A20)	The minimum value in the range A:A1..A:A20.
@avg(B2..B10)	The average of the values in the range B2..B10.
@sqrt(@sin(D1))	The square root of the sine of the value in cell D1.
@year(B10)	The year that corresponds to the date serial number in cell B10.
@std(<<DATA2>>A1..A20)	The standard deviation of the values in cells A1..A20 in the worksheet file DATA2.WK4.

continues

65

Table 11.1   Continued.

@Function	Result
@max(<<DATA2>>SALES)	The maximum value in the named range SALES in the worksheet file DATA2.WK4.

The following example demonstrates the use of an @function and shows you how to use POINT mode to specify a range address. The example assumes you want to display, in cell A5, the sum of the values in cells A1..A4.

1. Move the cell pointer to cell A5 and type @SUM(. (Stop after typing the open parenthesis.)

2. Use the up arrow key to move the cell pointer to cell A1. You are now in POINT mode, as indicated on the status bar.

3. Press the period key.

4. Use the down arrow key to move the cell pointer to cell A4. The highlight expands to cover A1..A4, and the range address is automatically entered into the @function in the contents line.

5. Type) (a closing parenthesis) to exit POINT mode. The cell pointer returns to cell A5, and the complete range address A1..A4 is entered in the @function in the contents line.

6. Press Enter. The @function is entered in cell A5, and displays its result.

Using the @Function Selector

The @function selector is the easiest way to enter @functions into a worksheet because it automatically provides the correct format, function name, and argument separators. Here's how to use the @function selector:

1. Move the cell pointer to the cell where you want to enter an @function.

2. Display the @function menu by clicking the @function selector (the @ button to the left of the contents box).

3. If the @function you want is listed on the menu, select it and proceed to step 7. If not, select List All to display the @Function List dialog box (Figure 11.1).

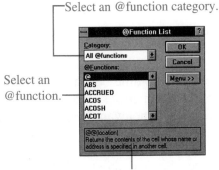

Select an @function category.

Select an @function.

Description of the highlighted @function

Figure 11.1   You can use the @Function List dialog box to enter @functions in your worksheet.

4. In the dialog box, select the desired category of @function from the Category drop-down box. To see a list of all @functions, select All @functions from the Category box.

5. Select an @function in the @Functions list. The dialog box displays a brief description of the selected @function.

6. To use the selected @function, click the OK button.

7. The selected @function is entered in the cell with placeholders for the required arguments. The first placeholder is highlighted.

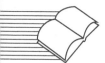

Argument Information that tells an @function how or what to calculate.

8. Replace each placeholder with the actual argument by typing a range address or range name, or by using POINT mode as described earlier in this lesson.

9. When all arguments are entered, press Enter or click on the Confirm button.

You should spend some time becoming familiar with 1-2-3 for Windows' @functions. They can be great timesavers. And you would not want to spend a lot of time writing a formula that duplicates an @function!

In this lesson, you learned about 1-2-3 for Windows built-in formulas, the @functions. In the next lesson, you'll learn how to change your worksheet's number and label format.

Lesson 12

Changing Number and Label Format

In this lesson, you'll learn how to control the way numbers and labels are displayed in your worksheet.

Why Worry About Format?

The term *format* refers to the way that numbers and labels are displayed in worksheet cells. Format does not affect the worksheet data, only its appearance. Through careful selection of worksheet format, you can improve the readability of your worksheets.

The Numeric Display Formats

1-2-3 for Windows offers a wide variety of ways to display numeric data. When you start a new worksheet, all cells have the default numeric format. You can modify this format with the **S**tyle **N**umber Format command. First, however, you need to become familiar with the various formats that are available. This section describes the formats you'll use most often.

Default Numeric Format The format used to display values in cells whose format has not been changed.

General format displays numbers with as many decimal places as needed, and displays negative numbers with a minus sign.

Value	Displayed As
106.99	106.99
–.015	–0.015

Fixed format is essentially the same as General format, but you specify the number of decimal places displayed (0–15). If the value has more decimal places than you specified, 1-2-3 automatically rounds the value for display (but the actual value with all its decimal places is still stored in the cell and is used in calculations).

Value	Displayed As	Decimal Places Specified
106.99	107.0	1
106.99	106.9900	4

Currency format displays numbers with a currency symbol, thousands separators, and 0–15 user-specified decimal places. Negative numbers are displayed in parentheses. *Comma format* is identical to Currency format except that no currency symbol is used.

Value	Currency Format Display	Comma Format Display	Decimal Places Specified
1000	$1,000	1,000	0
–50.95	($50.95)	(50.95)	2

Percent format displays numbers multiplied by 100, with a percent sign and 0–15 user-specified decimal places.

Value	Displayed As	Decimal Places Specified
0.15	15%	0
1.15	115.00%	2

Hidden format hides the data in the cell. You might use hidden format to protect sensitive data, such as salaries, from prying eyes. The cell appears blank, but when the cell pointer is on the cell, its data appears in the contents box. Use caution when applying Hidden format. Because the cell appears empty, you may inadvertently type in new data, overwriting the old.

Text format displays the text of formulas rather than the formula's results. Cells that contain values are displayed in General format. Use Text format to display formulas during worksheet debugging (when you're checking to see that formulas work properly).

Debugging The process of checking a worksheet for errors.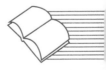

The *date and time formats* display date and time serial numbers in one of the available date or time formats. Here are examples of the five date formats:

Format	Example
Day-Month-Year	30-Jul-94
Day-Month	30-Jul
Month-Year	Jul-94
Long International	07/30/94
Short International	07/94

And the four time formats:

Format	Example
HH:MM:SS AM/PM	2:45:00 PM
HH:MM AM/PM	2:45 PM
Long International	14:45:00
Short International	14:45

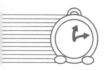

Format Display   At the left end of the status bar, 1-2-3 displays the name and, if applicable, the number of decimal places of the current cell's numeric format.

Automatic format is the numeric display format that is used unless you specify a different one. Automatic format displays numbers in Comma, Currency, Percent, or Scientific format, depending on the symbol you use when you enter the data. For example, if you enter a number followed by a percent sign it is displayed in Percent format. Automatic format attempts to guess what format is most appropriate for the data you enter.

Changing the Numeric Display Format

Each worksheet cell has its own numeric display format, which can be changed independently of all other worksheet cells. Changing display format has no effect on the data in the cell, only on how it is displayed. Initially, all cells have the default format, Automatic. To change the format of a range of cells, use the **S**tyle **N**umber Format command.

To change the numeric display format:

1. Highlight the range of the format you want to change.

2. Select **S**tyle **N**umber Format. Or you can click the range with the right mouse button, and then select Number Format from the quick menu. The Number Format dialog box is displayed (see Figure 12.1).

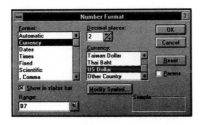

Figure 12.1   The Number Format dialog box.

3. Select the desired format from the list box.

4. If you select Fixed, Scientific, Currency, Comma, or Percent, the **D**ecimal Places text box appears. Click the up and down arrows or enter a value for the desired number of decimal places.

5. If you selected Currency format, a list of available currency symbols is displayed from which you can select.

6. Select OK. Numbers in the range are displayed in the selected format.

Quick Format　To quickly change a range's format or decimal places, click on the format or decimal place indicators on the status bar (see Figure 12.1).

Column Too Narrow?　If a number is too wide to be displayed in a cell, it is displayed as a row of asterisks. You can display the number properly by increasing the column width, as you'll learn in Lesson 13.

Changing Alignment

Alignment refers to the vertical and horizontal positioning of data in a cell. 1-2-3's default is to display labels aligned at the left and bottom of a cell, and to display values at the right and bottom of a cell. You can modify a range's vertical and horizontal alignment, and you can also apply some special alignment effects that can improve the appearance of your worksheets.

To change alignment:

1. Specify the range for which you want to change the alignment.

2. Select Style Alignment to display the Alignment dialog box (see Figure 12.2).

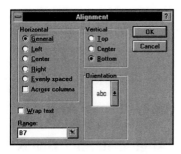

Figure 12.2   The Alignment dialog box.

3. Select a horizontal alignment option:

   - **General:** Labels are left aligned and values are right aligned.

   - **Left:** Data is aligned at the left edge of the cell.

   - **Center:** Data is centered in the cell.

   - **Right:** Data is aligned at the right edge of the cell.

   - **Evenly spaced:** Data is stretched out to fill the cell (does not affect labels ending with . ! ? or :).

4. Select Across Columns to align data in the leftmost cell across all the columns in the range (useful for centering labels over groups of columns).

5. Select a vertical alignment: Top, Center, or Bottom. The vertical alignment options are available only if the row height is larger than the row's largest font.

6. Select Wrap Text to have labels that are longer than the cell width displayed on more than one line (1-2-3 automatically adjusts the row height).

7. If you want to rotate the text in a cell, select an orientation from the Orientation drop-down box.

8. Click the OK button.

 **Alignment SmartIcons**   To quickly set left, right, or centered alignment, select the range and then click on the corresponding SmartIcon.

Changing the Default Display Format and Alignment

As mentioned earlier, the 1-2-3 for Windows defaults display numbers in Automatic format and display labels left-aligned. You can change these settings for the entire worksheet by following these steps:

1. Select Style Worksheet Defaults. The Worksheet Defaults dialog box is displayed (Figure 12.3).

Change format   Change alignment

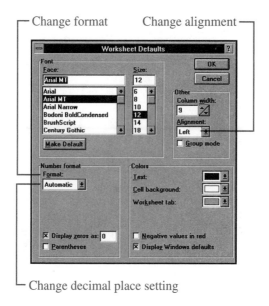

Change decimal place setting

Figure 12.3   The Worksheet Defaults dialog box.

2. To change the default label alignment, use the **A**lignment drop-down box to select Left, Center, or Right.

3. To change the default numeric display format, use the **F**ormat drop-down box and **D**ecimals text box to select the desired format.

4. Select OK.

In this lesson, you learned how to control the format and alignment used to display numbers and labels in your worksheet. The next lesson shows you how to change the size of worksheet rows and columns.

Lesson 13

Changing Column Width and Row Height

This lesson shows you how to control the height of rows and the width of columns in your worksheets.

Changing Column Width

All columns in 1-2-3 start out at a fixed width (usually 9 characters), but you will often find that changing the column width can improve readability of your worksheets. Labels that are too wide for a column will overlap columns to the right if those cells are empty. Otherwise, only a portion of the label will be displayed. Also, certain numeric formats will display a row of asterisks if the column is too narrow. Conversely, a column that is wider than needed for its contents will waste space on the screen. Figure 13.1 shows a worksheet that uses the default width for all columns.

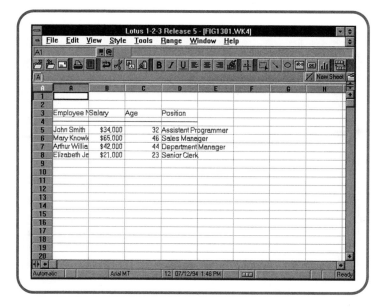

Figure 13.1 A worksheet with all columns at the default width.

Column width is specified in terms of characters in the default worksheet font size, which is 12 points. If you change a cell's font or font size (as you'll learn to do in Lesson 14), the actual number of characters that will be displayed may be greater or less than the set column width, depending on the new font size.

Every worksheet cell has a width that is determined by the width of the column it's in. You can adjust the width of each column in a worksheet. For example, Figure 13.2 shows a worksheet that uses different column widths that have been adjusted to suit the worksheet data.

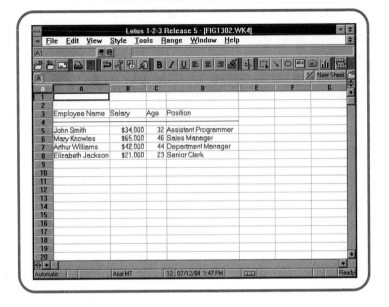

Figure 13.2 A worksheet with column widths adjusted to suit the data.

The easiest way to change the width of a single column is with the mouse:

1. Move the mouse pointer into the worksheet frame that contains the column letters.

2. Point at the right border of the column being changed. The mouse pointer changes into a double-headed arrow.

3. Press and hold the mouse button, drag the column to the desired width, and then release the mouse button.

To specify an exact column width, or if you don't have a mouse, you must use the **S**tyle **C**olumn Width command:

1. Highlight a range that includes at least one cell in each column you want to adjust. For example, to change the width of columns A through C you could select the range A4..C4.

2. Select **S**tyle **C**olumn Width. The Column Width dialog box is displayed (see Figure 13.3).

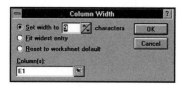

Figure 13.3 Column Width dialog box.

3. To specify column width in characters, select the Set width to option. Click the arrows or enter a value to specify the column width in the characters text box.

4. To automatically set the column width to fit its widest entry, select the Fit Widest Entry option.

5. If you want to reset the columns to the default column width, select **R**eset to Worksheet Default.

6. Select OK.

Wide Load To quickly fit the width of a single column to its widest entry, double-click on the right border of the column's letter in the worksheet frame.

As you saw earlier in this lesson, all columns have the same width unless you change them. This width is known as the *global column width*. Global column width starts out at 9 characters, but you can change the global column width by following these steps. (You don't need to select specific cells or a range to change the global column width.)

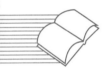

Global Column Width The worksheet's default column width.

1. Select Style Worksheet Defaults.

2. In the Worksheet Defaults dialog box, type a value or click the arrows to enter the desired width in the Column width text box.

3. Select OK.

Changing Row Height

The 1-2-3 for Windows default is to set the height of each row to accommodate the largest font in that row. Normally the default row height is 14 points. You can adjust row height manually as well. Row height is specified in points, where 72 points equal one inch. (This method is used because, as you'll see in the next lesson, font size is also measured in points.)

To change the height of a single row with the mouse:

1. Move the mouse pointer into the worksheet frame that contains the row numbers.

2. Point at the row border below the row being changed, and the mouse pointer changes to a double-headed arrow.

3. Press and hold the mouse button, drag the row to the desired height, and release the mouse button.

To change row height to a specific value, or if you don't have a mouse, you must use the **S**tyle **R**ow Height command:

1. Highlight a range that includes at least one cell in each row. For example, to change the height of rows 2 through 4 you could select the range A2..A4.

2. Select Style Row Height. The Row Height dialog box is displayed (see Figure 13.4).

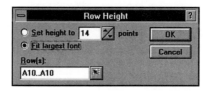

Figure 13.4   Row Height dialog box.

3. If it is not already selected, select the Set height to text box and enter the desired height in the text box.

4. Select OK, and the specified rows change to the new height.

Change Your Mind? If you decide you want to return the rows to the default height (that of the largest font in the row), simply select Fit Largest Font in step 3 above.

In this lesson, you learned how to control the width and height of worksheet columns and rows. The next lesson shows you how to use fonts and borders to enhance the appearance of your worksheets.

Lesson 14

Using Fonts, Borders, and Styles

This lesson shows you how to use fonts, borders, and frames to enhance your worksheets.

Changing the Font

By using different *fonts*, you can increase the clarity and visual appeal of your worksheets and printouts. Some of the fonts available in 1-2-3 for Windows are shown in Figure 14.1. The exact fonts you have available will depend on your Windows installation and your printer. Each font has a name that identifies the type style, such as Arial, Helvetica, or Times Roman. Each font is usually available in several different sizes, which are measured in points (72 points equal one inch). You can add special attributes, such as boldface, italics, and underlining, to any font.

Font   A set of characters that have the same typeface and type size. For example, Helvetica 12-point is a font. Helvetica is the typeface, and 12-point is the size.

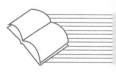

Bold SmartIcon   Italics SmartIcon   Underline SmartIcon

Style button

Figure 14.1   Some of 1-2-3 for Windows' fonts.

To change the font used to display and print a range of cells:

1. Highlight the range in which you want to change the font.

2. Select Style Font & Attributes. The Font & Attributes dialog box is displayed (see Figure 14.2).

86

Choose a font name. Choose a font size.

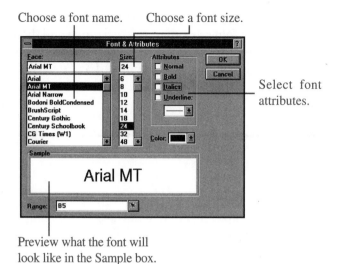

Select font
attributes.

Preview what the font will
look like in the Sample box.

Figure 14.2   The Font & Attributes dialog box.

3. Select the desired font name from the Face list box.

4. Select the desired font size from the Size list box.

5. If desired, select the Bold, Italics, and/or Underline
   attributes (or select Normal to turn all attributes off). If
   you select Underline, choose an underline style from
   the drop-down box.

6. Use the Color drop-down box to select a font color.

7. Look in the Sample box to see how the selected font and
   attributes will appear.

8. Select OK. The range is displayed in the selected font.
   Row heights are adjusted, if necessary, to accommodate larger fonts.

Changing Font Attributes   To quickly add or remove font attributes, select a range and then click on the B (Bold), I (Italics), or U (Underline) SmartIcons shown in Figure 14.1.

Changing the Default Worksheet Font

1-2-3 uses the default font for all cells whose font hasn't been changed. You can change the default font and its size by following these steps:

1. Select Style Worksheet Defaults.

2. In the dialog box, the current default font name is given in the Face text box. Select a new font name from the list.

3. If desired, select the default font size from the Size list.

4. Click OK.

The new default font will be used for all cells except those whose font you have explicitly changed.

Adding Borders and Frames

You can add borders and frames to your worksheet cells. Borders are effective for setting different data areas off from one another, and frames can be used to add emphasis to a worksheet or printed report.

When adding borders to a range, you have the following placement options:

- **O**utline places a border around the outer edge of the entire range.

- **All** places a border around each individual cell in the range.

- **L**eft, **R**ight, **T**op, and Botto**m** place a line at the specified edge of each cell in the range.

To remove borders and/or a frame from a range, highlight the range, display the Lines & Color dialog box, and turn off the appropriate check boxes.

To add borders or a frame to a worksheet range:

1. Select the range of cells.

2. Select **S**tyle **L**ines & Color to display the Lines & Color dialog box (see Figure 14.3).

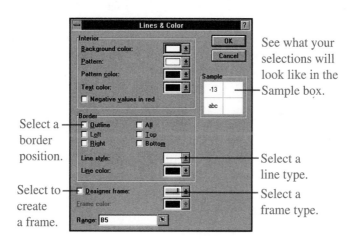

Figure 14.3   The Lines & Color dialog box.

3. In the Border section of the dialog box, turn on the check box for each location where you want a border in the range.

4. A sample line is displayed next to each selected border option. To change border line style or color, select the Line style and Line color drop-down boxes and choose a style and color.

5. To add a frame to the range, turn on the Designer frame check box and select a frame from the drop-down box. Select a frame color from the Color drop-down box.

6. Select OK. The range is displayed with the selected borders and/or frame.

Using Named Styles

A *named style* is a set of formatting commands that has been saved and assigned a name. You can use named styles to quickly and consistently apply the same formatting to different worksheet areas. 1-2-3 has ten predefined named styles, and you can also create your own. A named style can include number format, colors, patterns, font and attributes, borders, frames, and alignment. You can have a maximum of 16 named styles.

To create a named style:

1. Highlight a worksheet range or cell that has the formatting you want assigned to the style.

2. Select Style Named Style to display the Named Style dialog box (see Figure 14.4).

3. Enter the style name in the Style **n**ame text box. The name can be up to 15 characters long.

4. Select Define and then choose OK.

Select to delete a style name from the list.

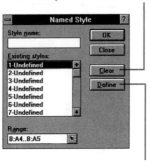

Select to add a style name to the list.

Figure 14.4   The Named Style dialog box.

To assign a style to a worksheet range:

1. Highlight the range.

2. Select Style Named Style to display the Named Style dialog box.

3. Select the desired style name from the **E**xisting Styles list.

4. Click OK.

Fast Styles   To quickly assign a style, highlight the range, click the Style button on the status bar (to the left of the Font indicator), and then click the desired style name. Figure 14.1 shows the Style button.

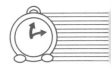

In this lesson, you learned how to enhance your worksheets with fonts, borders, and frames. You also learned how to use named styles. In the next lesson, you'll learn how to print your worksheet.

Lesson 15

Printing Your Worksheet

This lesson shows you how to create printouts of your worksheet data.

Printing with the Default Settings

A worksheet printout can be as simple as a single column of numbers for your own reference, or a multi-page, formatted document for distribution in your company. Creating a printout of your worksheet using the default print settings is very easy.

Printing a Worksheet   To print, you must have installed a printer in Microsoft Windows. The printer must be connected to your system, turned on, and on-line. See your Windows reference manual for details.

To print all or part of a worksheet using the default print settings, follow these steps:

1. To print part of a worksheet, highlight the range to print.

2. Select File Print or click on the Print SmartIcon. The Print dialog box is displayed, as shown in Figure 15.1.

Select to change the way the page will appear.

Choose the print range.

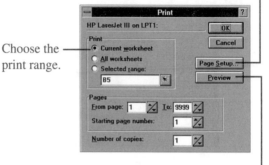

Select to view the range before it's printed.

Figure 15.1   The Print dialog box.

3. In the Print box, select the desired option:

- Current **w**orksheet prints all data in the current worksheet.

- **A**ll worksheets prints all worksheets in the current worksheet file.

- Selected **r**ange prints the current selection

4. Select OK. The data is printed.

Previewing a Print Job

The 1-2-3 screen shows a close approximation of what a printout will look like. Fonts, outlines, frames, and so on are similar in the printout to what you see in your worksheet.

For an exact preview of the way the printout will look, you can use 1-2-3 for Windows' Print Preview feature.

To view a screen preview of a print job:

1. If you'll be printing part of a worksheet, highlight the range to preview.

2. Select File Print Preview or click on the Preview SmartIcon. The Print Preview dialog box is displayed.

3. In the Preview section, select the area to be previewed: Current worksheet, All worksheets, or Selected range.

4. Select OK. The first page of the printout is displayed on the Print Preview screen (see Figure 15.2).

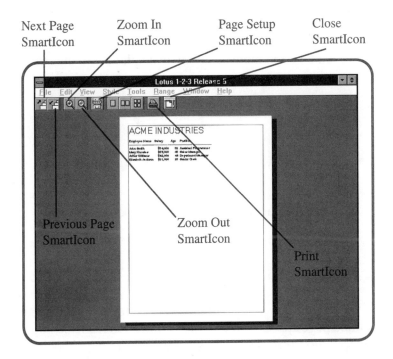

Figure 15.2 The Print Preview window with a page displayed.

While the Print Preview screen is displayed, you can perform the following actions:

- Click on the Next Page SmartIcon or press Enter to view the next page.

- Click on the Previous Page SmartIcon or press PgUp to view the previous page.

- Click on the Zoom Out SmartIcon or press the minus sign on the numeric keypad to zoom out (make the page smaller).

- Click on the Zoom In SmartIcon or press the plus sign on the numeric keypad to zoom in (make the page larger). While you are zoomed in, use the arrow keys to view different sections of the page.

- Click on the Single, Facing or Multiple Pages SmartIcon to change the number of pages displayed on the Print Preview screen.

- Click on the Page Setup SmartIcon to change the page setup (see below).

- Click on the Print SmartIcon to print.

- Click the Close SmartIcon or press Esc to close the Print Preview screen and return to the worksheet.

Changing Page Setup

You use *Page Setup* to change the way certain aspects of the printed page appear. Page setup is controlled from the Page Setup dialog box, shown in Figure 15.3. You display this dialog box by selecting File Page Setup, by clicking the Page Setup button in either the Print or Print Preview dialog boxes, or by clicking the Page Setup SmartIcon on the Print Preview screen.

Enter a header or footer or use an Insert SmartIcon.

Change margin settings.

Insert SmartIcons.

Save page settings.

Change page orientation.

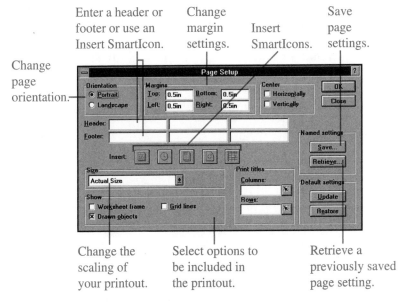

Change the scaling of your printout.

Select options to be included in the printout.

Retrieve a previously saved page setting.

Figure 15.3 The Page Setup dialog box.

Setting Margins

The *margin* is the width of blank paper left between the printed area and the edge of the page. The default margins are 0.50 inch top, left, and right, and 0.55 inch bottom. To change the margin, enter a new value in the corresponding text box in the Page Setup dialog box. To specify the margin in inches, type **in** for *inches* after the value. For centimeters or millimeters, follow the value with **cm** or **mm**.

Changing Size

You can change the scaling of your printouts so that more or less data can fit on a page. This is different from changing the point size of the lettering, but it accomplishes much the same result. You can select the following options from the Size drop-down box in the Page Setup dialog box:

- *Actual Size* prints data at its normal full size (this is the default).

- *Fit all to page* automatically sizes the data to fit all of it on a single page.

- *Fit columns to page* automatically sizes the data to fit all columns on a single page.

- *Fit rows to page* automatically sizes the data to fit all rows on a single page.

- *Manually scale* lets you specify an exact size. To compress the print range, enter a percentage factor between 15 and 99. To expand the print range, enter a percentage factor between 101 and 1000. For example, 50 compresses to half normal size, while 200 expands to double normal size.

Setting Orientation

Orientation lets you control the way data is oriented on the page. There are two page orientation options:

- **Portrait** (the default) prints the data with worksheet rows parallel to the short edge of the paper.

- Landscape prints the data with worksheet rows parallel to the long edge of the paper. (This mode is not available on all printers.)

To set orientation, click on either the Landscape or Portrait option button in the Page Setup dialog box (Figure 15.3).

Printing Wide Worksheets   Use landscape orientation and the Fit all to page Size option to fit wide worksheet ranges on single pages.

Headers and Footers

Headers and footers are text that is printed at the top or bottom of every page. To add a header or footer to your 1-2-3 printout, type the desired text in the **H**eader or **F**ooter text boxes in the Page Setup dialog box. There are three text boxes each for header and footer. Text you type in the left boxes will be left-aligned on the page; text you type in the center boxes will be centered on the page; and text you type in the right boxes will be right-aligned on the page.

While entering text in the **H**eader or **F**ooter text boxes, you can click the Insert SmartIcons to add the following five items to the header or footer:

   The current date.

   The current time.

   The page number.

The worksheet file name.

 The contents of a worksheet cell. (Click on the icon and then enter the cell's address.)

Other Print Options

In the Page Setup dialog box, you can select one or more of these options in the Show section:

• The **G**rid lines option prints the worksheet grid (the vertical and horizontal lines between cells).

• The **W**orksheet frame option prints the worksheet frame (the row numbers and column letters) on each page.

• The Drawn **O**bject option prints objects you have drawn on the worksheet. (Lesson 19 shows you how to draw objects on a worksheet.)

Saving Print Settings

Once you have set the page setup options, you can save them with an assigned name. Then you can retrieve the settings later for use in another print job. To save page setup settings:

1. Choose the Save button in the Page Setup dialog box to display the Save Named Settings dialog box.

2. Enter a 1–8 character name in the File **n**ame text box.

3. Click OK.

To retrieve named page settings you saved previously:

1. Choose the Retrieve button in the Page Setup dialog box to display the Retrieve Named Settings dialog box.

2. Select a named setting from the files list box, or type the settings name in the File name text box.

3. Click OK.

In this lesson, you learned how to create printouts of your worksheets and how to control printing options. In the next lesson, you'll learn how to create a basic graph.

Creating and Printing a Chart

In this lesson, you'll learn how to create a chart from your worksheet data and how to print it.

Chart Basics

A *chart* is a visual representation of numerical data, and can be a very effective tool for summarizing numerical information. To use charts effectively, you must be familiar with the parts of a chart. Figure 16.1 shows a 1-2-3 for Windows chart with its components labeled. Every 1-2-3 for Windows chart contains some or all of these components.

Charts are displayed in the worksheet at a location you specify. A displayed chart may appear to cover up worksheet data, but the data is still there—it's just hidden. You can move the chart to see the data.

All 1-2-3 charts work with *data series*. A data series is a group of labels or values in your worksheet that are usually together in the same row or column. There is one X data series, and there can be between 1 and 23 Y data series. The X data series is plotted on the chart's X axis and usually contains labels that serve to identify the data by category (for example, Month, Sales Region, State, and so on). The Y data series are plotted on the Y axis and always contain numbers, or values.

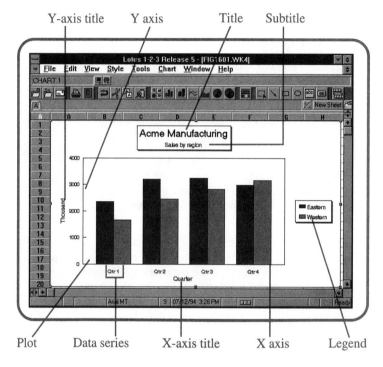

Figure 16.1 The components of a chart.

Chart Types

1-2-3 for Windows offers a variety of different chart types. When creating a chart, you select the type depending on your data and the point you are trying to make. Table 16.1 summarizes the available chart types.

Table 16.1 1-2-3 for Windows' chart types.

Type	Description
Line	Plots each data value as a point or symbol, and connects the data points in each data series with a line. Suited for illustrating changes that occur over time.
Area	A line chart in which data series are plotted stacked on each other, and the regions between plots are filled with a color or pattern. Use an area chart to illustrate trends over time when you want to show overall totals as well as the contribution of each series to the totals.
Bar	Displays numerical values as a set of vertical rectangular bars along the X axis. The height of each bar is proportional to the corresponding value. Appropriate for comparing totals for several categories.
Pie	Plots only a single Y data series. The plot is a circle, with the entire circle representing the total of all values in the data series. The circle is divided into wedges; the size of each wedge represents the percentage that the corresponding value contributes toward the total.
XY	Sometimes called a scatter chart. This is the only chart type that plots values on the X axis. Used to display the relationship, or correlation, between two or more sets of numerical values.
HLCO	High-low-close-open. A specialized kind of chart used for stock market data.
Mixed	Combines bar, line, and/or area chart types in one chart.
Radar	A line chart wrapped around a central point. Useful for showing the uniformity or symmetry of data.
3D Line	A line chart displayed in a three-dimensional perspective.

Type	Description
3D Area	An area chart displayed with a three-dimensional perspective.
3D Bar	Identical to a bar chart except that each individual bar is given three-dimensional perspective and appears solid.
3D Pie	A regular pie chart in three-dimensional perspective.

Creating a Default Chart

There are three steps involved in creating a chart:

1. Select the data to be charted.

2. Specify the type of chart.

3. Enhance the chart with titles, legends, and other additions. (This step is optional and will be covered in the next lesson.)

Selecting the data to be charted means selecting one or more data series, which you learned about at the beginning of this lesson. The data series is a single row or column of values that appears as a plot in the chart. A chart contains between one and 23 Y series, identified by the letters A through W. Values in each Y series are plotted against the chart's Y axis (or, in pie charts, as wedges). A chart also contains one X series, which consists of labels or values that are plotted on the chart's X axis.

Let's look at an example. Figure 16.2 shows a worksheet that contains some data to be charted. We want to create a bar chart that shows the relative contribution to sales of the Eastern and Western regions for each of the four quarters. Here's how to do it.

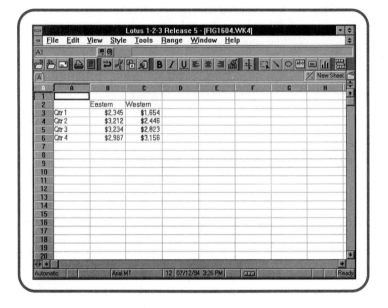

Figure 16.2 The worksheet data to be charted.

1. Highlight the range to be charted (A2..C6 in the example).

2. Select Tools Chart. The mouse pointer changes to a small chart symbol.

3. Click the location where you want the upper left corner of the chart. 1-2-3 creates a default size bar chart, as shown in Figure 16.3.

You Say You Want a Custom Size Chart? To create a custom size chart (as opposed to default size), instead of step 3, point at one corner of the area where you want the chart, drag diagonally to the opposite corner, and release the mouse button.

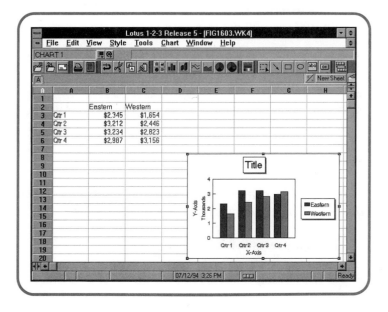

Figure 16.3 The default size bar chart.

How Default Charts Are Made

When you create a chart as described above, 1-2-3 follows certain rules in deciding how to interpret the data in the highlighted range. The rules are designed so that 1-2-3 can guess as accurately as possible how you want the chart to appear. The rules depend on the relative number of rows and columns in the highlighted range.

If the range contains more rows than columns, the data is grouped into data series by columns:

* The first column is the X series.

* Second and subsequent columns are the Y series (A, B, and so on).

* If there are labels at the top of the Y range columns, they are used for the legend labels.

* Blank rows and columns are ignored.

If the range contains more columns than rows (or an equal number), the data is grouped into data series by rows:

* The first row is the X series.

* Second and subsequent rows are the Y series (A, B, and so on).

* If there are labels at the left of the Y range rows, they are used for the legend labels.

* Blank rows and columns are ignored.

If the selected range contains labels above or to the left of the numeric data, 1-2-3 uses the labels to create the title, subtitle, and legend labels. For example, the chart shown in Figure 16.4 was created by highlighting the range A3..C9.

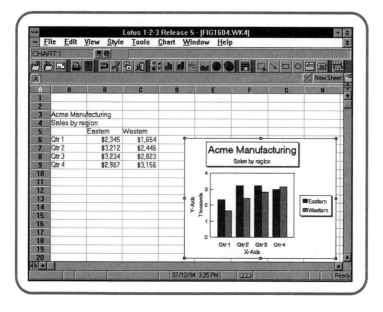

Figure 16.4   If the selected range includes labels above or to the left of the numeric data, 1-2-3 uses those labels for the chart titles and legend.

Changing Chart Type

1-2-3's default is to produce a bar chart. Once you have a chart on-screen, you can change it to a different type by performing these steps:

1. Select the chart by clicking on it. A selected chart displays small black rectangles on its border.

2. On the main menu, the **R**ange menu changes to Chart when a chart is selected.

3. Select Chart Type to display the Type dialog box (see Figure 16.5).

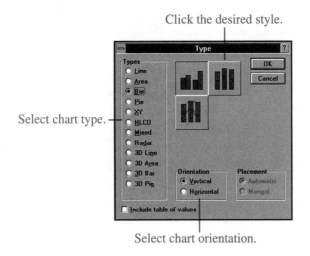

Click the desired style.

Select chart type.

Select chart orientation.

Figure 16.5   The Type dialog box.

4. In the Type box, select the desired chart type.

5. Select the desired chart orientation, Horizontal or Vertical.

6. The dialog box displays small samples of the available styles for the selected chart type and orientation. Click the desired style.

7. Click OK.

Moving and Resizing a Chart

You can quickly move a chart to a new location, or change its size and proportions. To move a chart, follow these steps:

1. Select the chart by clicking on it. A selected chart displays small black rectangles on its border.

2. Select Edit Cut, press Ctrl+X, or click the Cut SmartIcon.

3. Move the cell pointer to the location where you want the top left corner of the chart.

4. Select Edit Paste, press Ctrl+V, or click the Paste SmartIcon.

   To change a chart's size:

1. Select the chart as described in the previous steps.

2. Point the mouse at one of the small black rectangles on the chart's border. The mouse pointer will change into a four-headed arrow.

3. Press the mouse button and drag the chart outline to the desired size and shape.

4. Release the mouse button.

Deleting a Chart   To delete a chart, select it and then press Del.

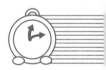

Saving Charts

You don't need to take any special action to save your charts. All the charts you have defined are automatically saved with the worksheet file when you save it.

Printing Charts

If you print all or part of a worksheet (as you learned in Lesson 15), any charts in the worksheet will be printed along with the worksheet data. To print just a chart, follow these steps:

1. Select the chart.

2. Select File Print or click the Print SmartIcon.

3. In the Print dialog box, be sure that the Selected chart option button is on.

4. Select OK.

In this lesson, you learned the basics of creating a chart. The next lesson shows you how to enhance a chart.

Enhancing a Chart

In this lesson, you'll learn how to add enhancements to your charts.

Chart Enhancements

The previous lesson showed you how to create a basic chart. You will usually want to add enhancements to the chart. Enhancements consist of various additions and modifications to a chart that improve its appearance, clarity, and impact. This lesson introduces the most important chart enhancements.

Adding Chart Titles and Footnotes

You can add a title, subtitle, and footnotes to a 1-2-3 for Windows chart. The title is displayed centered above the chart, and the subtitle is displayed centered below the title. Footnotes are additional explanatory text displayed below the chart. Figure 17.1 illustrates titles and footnotes. As you learned in the previous lesson, 1-2-3 can automatically add a title to a chart if you include label cells in the data range to be charted. Or you can add titles manually after you've created a chart. The following instructions will tell you how.

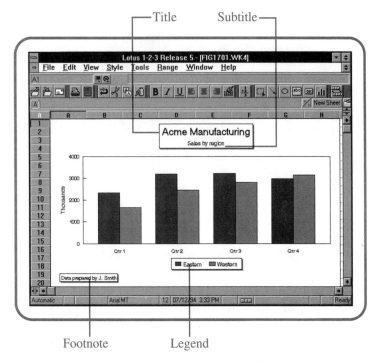

Figure 17.1 A chart with titles, a footnote, and a legend.

To add or modify titles and/or footnotes:

1. Select the chart by clicking on its border. Remember, the chart displays small black boxes on its border when it is selected.

2. Select Chart Headings to display the Headings dialog box (see Figure 17.2).

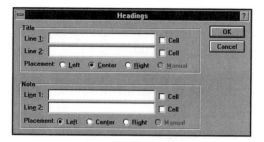

Figure 17.2 The Headings dialog box.

3. Enter the main title and subtitle text in the Line **1** and Line **2** text boxes in the Title section of the dialog box. To use the contents of a worksheet cell as a title, turn on the Cell check box and enter the cell address or range name in the text box.

4. Specify title placement by clicking the Left, Center, or Right option button. The Manual button is on if you previously moved the title manually (as will be described at the end of this lesson).

5. To enter a footnote, repeat steps 3 and 4 in the Note section.

6. Click OK.

Adding a Legend

A *legend* is a key that identifies a chart's data ranges by the color, pattern, or symbol used to plot them (as shown in Figure 17.1). Charts that include more than one data range usually need a legend. As you learned in the previous lesson, 1-2-3 can automatically create a legend from row or

115

column headings that are included in the chart's data range. In some cases, you may need to add a legend manually, or modify the automatic legend.

Legend   A key that identifies the data plotted in a chart.

To add or modify a legend:

1. Select the chart by clicking on it.

2. Double-click the legend or select Chart Legend to display the Legend dialog box (see Figure 17.3).

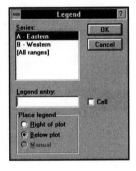

Figure 17.3   The Legend dialog box.

3. In the Series list box, select a data series.

4. In the Legend entry text box, enter the legend label for the selected data series. To use the contents of a cell as a legend, turn on the Cell check box and enter the cell address in the text box.

5. Repeat steps 3 and 4 for any additional data series.

6. Select a legend placement option under Place legend.

7. Select OK.

If the worksheet contains labels in adjacent cells that you want to use for the legend, you can quickly assign them as legend labels:

1. Display the Legend dialog box as described earlier.

2. In the Series list box, select [All Ranges].

3. In the Legend entry box, enter the range address of the worksheet cells that contain the legend labels.

4. Click OK. The labels in the specified range are assigned to the data ranges in top-to-bottom or left-to-right order.

Moving Chart Titles, Footnotes, and Legends

The easiest way to move a chart's titles, footnotes, or legend is by dragging. Here are the steps to follow:

1. Point at the chart element that you want to move.

2. Press and hold the left mouse button.

3. Drag to the new location. As you drag, the mouse pointer changes to a small hand, and an outline of the chart element moves with it.

4. When the outline is in the desired position, release the mouse button.

You can also move the chart's titles, notes, or legend to a predefined position. Simply display the Headings dialog box or the Legend dialog box, and then select the desired placement option.

In this lesson, you learned how to add some enhancements to your charts. The next lesson shows you how to use some additional chart enhancements.

More Chart Enhancements

In this lesson, you'll learn how to use some additional chart enhancements.

Adding Axis Titles

You can add a title to each axis on the chart to identify the data being illustrated. The X-axis title is displayed below the X axis, and the Y-axis title is displayed vertically next to the axis. You can enter a title from the keyboard, or you can use a label in a worksheet cell as a title. Figure 18.1 shows a chart with an axis title and a *unit title*.

Unit Title   A unit title describes the numerical units on a chart axis.

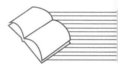

To add or modify an axis title:

1. Select the chart by clicking on it.

2. Select Chart Axis. Then select either X-Axis or Y-Axis to display the X-Axis or Y-Axis dialog box (see Figure 18.2).

119

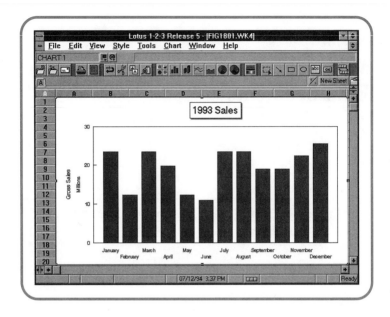

Figure 18.1 A chart with an axis title and a unit title.

Figure 18.2 The Y-Axis dialog box.

3. Enter the desired title in the Axis title text box. To use a label in a worksheet cell as the title, turn on the Cell check box and then enter the cell's address or range name in the Axis title text box.

4. Select OK.

Quick Axis Display   To quickly display the X-
Axis or Y-Axis dialog box, double-click the corresponding axis title on the chart.

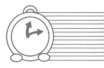

Changing Axis Scale

The term *axis scale* refers to the increment at which numbers are displayed on an axis. You can control the range of
values (the maximum and minimum values on the axis) and
the type of axis scale. For example, you could use logarithmic scale to plot a range of data that includes both very large
and very small values. The three types of axis scales are:

- Standard scale, in which axis numbers change in a
  linear fashion.

- Logarithmic scale, in which axis numbers change loga-
  rithmically.

- 100% scale, in which the values range from 0% to 100%
  and represent percentages instead of absolute values.

Axis scale is applicable only to the Y axis on most
charts. The one exception is the XY chart, where axis scale
is applicable to both the X axis and the Y axis. 1-2-3's
default is to use a standard scale and to set the axis range to
suit the largest and smallest values in the data being plotted.
You can change axis scale by following these steps:

1. Double-click the title of the axis you want to change, or
   select the chart and then select Chart Axis X-Axis or
   Chart Axis Y-Axis to display the corresponding dialog
   box (see Figure 18.2).

2. To change the type of scale, select Options. Then choose the type of scale from the Type of scale drop-down box and choose OK.

3. To change the axis range, turn on the Upper limit and Lower limit check boxes and then enter the desired axis limits in the text boxes.

4. Click OK.

The Scale Is All Wrong To return an axis to automatic scaling, display the X-axis or Y-axis dialog box and turn off the Upper limit and Lower limit check boxes.

Changing Axis Unit Titles

The unit title identifies the type of unit plotted on the axis: thousands, units, miles per hour, and so on. Unit titles can also scale the axis units by some exponent of 10 to make the chart clearer. For example, if the values you are plotting are in the range 1,000,000 to 10,000,000, you could use an exponent of 6 (10 to the 6th power = 1,000,000) and a unit title of "millions." This is shown in Figure 18.1. An axis unit title is displayed between the axis title and the axis. You can have 1-2-3 automatically decide on an exponent and unit title, or you can do it yourself.

To add or modify unit titles:

1. Double-click the title of the axis to which you want to add a unit title. Or select the chart and then select Chart Axis X-Axis or Chart Axis Y-Axis to display the corresponding axis dialog box.

2. Choose Options to display the Options dialog box (Figure 18.3).

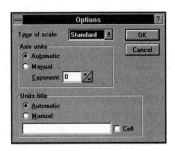

Figure 18.3   The Options dialog box.

3. Under Axis units:

   • Select Automatic to have 1-2-3 determine the exponent.

   • Select Manual and enter an exponent in the text box to set the exponent yourself.

4. Under Units title:

   • Select Automatic to have 1-2-3 create a unit title based on the exponent used.

   • Select Manual to enter your own unit title in the text box (or click on Cell and enter a cell address).

5. Select OK.

In this lesson you learned how to control some advanced chart options. In the next lesson you'll learn how to add graphics to your worksheet.

Lesson 19
Using Graphics

In this lesson, you'll learn how to add graphics to your worksheets.

What Are Graphics?

A *graphic* is an object that you draw in your 1-2-3 worksheet. You can draw a variety of lines, arrows, shapes and text blocks. Graphics can be used to enhance the appearance of a worksheet and to call attention to important data. You can add graphics anywhere, including on a chart. When you print a worksheet or a chart, the graphics are printed as well. Figure 19.1 shows a worksheet that contains some graphics.

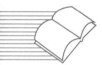 **Graphic** An object (such as an arrow, line, or box) that you draw on your worksheet.

 **Graphic SmartIcons** Many of the graphics drawing commands are represented by SmartIcons that are displayed when a chart is selected.

124

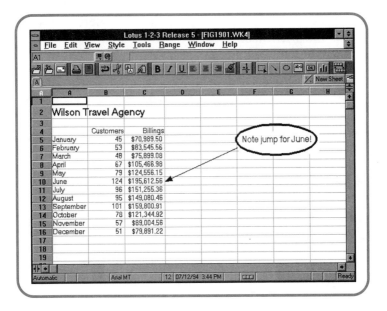

Figure 19.1 Graphics can be used to enhance a worksheet.

Drawing Lines, Arcs, and Arrows

You can add arrows to your worksheet to call attention to important points. Lines and arcs can also be used to create shapes of many types. To create a line, arc, or arrow:

1. Select Tools Draw and select Line, Arc, or Arrow.

2. Move the mouse pointer to the position where you want the graphic to begin.

3. Press and hold the mouse button and drag to the end of the object:

- For an arrow, drag toward the end where you want the arrowhead.

- For an arc, drag in the direction that you want the arc to curve.

4. Release the mouse button.

Drawing Rectangles and Ellipses

You can add rectangles, rounded rectangles, and ellipses to your worksheet.

1. Select Tools Draw and select Rectangle, Rounded Rectangle, or Ellipse.

2. Move the mouse pointer to the worksheet location where you want the shape to begin.

3. Press the mouse button and drag. As you do, a dotted outline expands to show the object's size.

4. Release the mouse button.

Drawing Circles and Squares   To draw a circle instead of an ellipse, or a square instead of a rectangle, hold down Shift while you drag.

Creating a Text Block

A *text block* is a rectangular section of text that can be placed anywhere on a worksheet. You can use text blocks to create notes and captions that point out and explain worksheet data. Figure 19.2 shows a worksheet that contains a text block. To create a text block:

1. Select Tools Draw Text

2. Move the mouse to point at the location where you want the text block to begin.

3. Click to create a default size text block. Drag across the worksheet to create a custom size text block.

4. Release the mouse button. An empty text block appears with a blinking vertical cursor in it.

5. Enter the text you want in the text block.

6. When you are finished, click outside the text block.

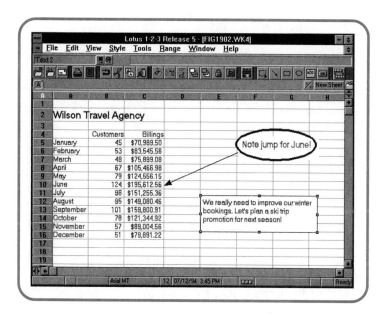

Figure 19.2 A text block can be used to put notes and captions in your worksheets.

Modifying Graphic Objects

To modify a graphic object you must first select it by clicking on it. When a graphic object is selected, small squares called *handles* are displayed on the object's borders. With the graphic object selected, you can work with it in these ways:

- To delete the object, press Del.

- To move the object, point anywhere on the object except the handles and drag it to the new location.

- To change the object's size, point at one of its handles and drag the outline to the desired size.

   To make a copy of a graphic object:

1. Select the graphic object.

2. Select Edit Copy.

3. Move the cell pointer to a cell where you want the copy placed. The cell can be in a different worksheet or worksheet file.

4. Select Edit Paste.

Modifying Lines and Colors

You can modify the color of any graphic object, and you can also change the pattern and thickness of its lines and other aspects of its appearance. Here are the steps to follow:

1. Click on the object with the right mouse button to display the quick menu.

2. Select Lines & Color from the quick menu to display the Lines & Color dialog box.

3. Make the desired selections in the dialog box.

4. Click OK.

The content of the Lines & Color dialog box varies depending on the type of graphic object you have selected. For example, Figure 19.3 shows the dialog box that is displayed if you have selected either an arrow or a line. Use the dialog box elements in the following manner:

- Use the **St**yle drop-down box to select a line style (solid, dotted, dashed, and so on).

- Use the **W**idth drop-down box to select a line width.

- Use the **C**olor drop-down box to select a color.

- Use the **A**rrowhead drop-down box to select positions for arrowheads on the line.

- View the effect of your selection in the Sample box.

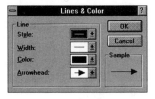

Figure 19.3   The Lines & Color dialog box.

Making a Graphic Object Transparent

1-2-3's default is for rectangles, rounded rectangles, ellipses, and text blocks to cover whatever is behind them, whether it be worksheet data or part of a chart. You can make these graphic objects transparent, permitting whatever is behind them to show through. To make a graphic object transparent:

1. Select the object.

2. Select Style Lines & Color.

3. In the dialog box, display the Pattern drop-down box.

4. Select the pattern block with the "T" in the center.

5. Click OK.

In this lesson, you learned how to add graphics to your worksheets. The next lesson shows you how to create a 1-2-3 database.

Lesson 20
Creating a Database

In this lesson, you'll learn how to create a database.

Database Fundamentals

A *database* is a collection of similar information with a uniform structure. Familiar database examples include mailing lists, merchandise inventories, and checkbook registers. In a hardware store's merchandise inventory database, for example, each entry, or item, has the same structure: part name, part number, cost, quantity on hand, and so on.

Part name	Part number	Cost	Quantity on hand
Hammer	BN-654	$5.49	13
Wrench	HX-121	$8.85	8
Pliers	CV-413	$4.49	17

You need to know the following terms to understand 1-2-3 for Windows' databases. A *record* is one complete database entry. In the preceding example, the information

131

about each tool comprises one record. A *field* is an item of information contained in each record. In our example, there are four fields: part name, part number, cost, and quantity on hand.

The row and column structure of a 1-2-3 for Windows worksheet is ideal for a database. Each field has its own column, and each record has its own row. The top row of a 1-2-3 database contains the field names, which are unique names identifying the database fields. (Field names must be labels.)

The term *database table* refers to a rectangular range in a worksheet that contains information organized in this manner. Figure 20.1 shows a small 1-2-3 for Windows database table.

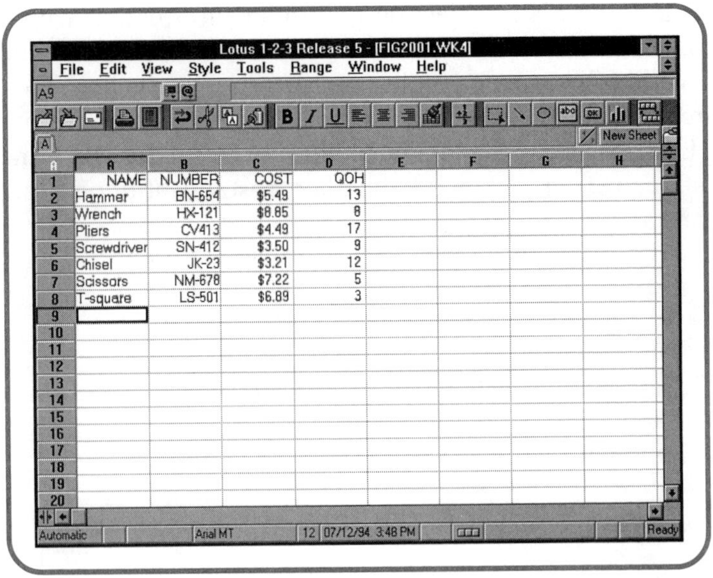

Figure 20.1 A 1-2-3 for Windows database table.

There's only one restriction on the data that can be put in a database table. All the entries in a given field should be of the same data type: values or labels. 1-2-3 for Windows will not prevent you from entering inconsistent data types in a database field. But if you do, unexpected results may occur later during certain database operations, such as searching and sorting.

Creating a Database Table

It's a good idea to do some planning before you create a database table. You need to decide the following points:

- What information will the database table include? For example, does a mailing list need a separate field for Country or will it contain only domestic addresses?

- How will fields be ordered left-to-right in the database table?

- What field names will be used? You must use a unique name for each field, and they should be descriptive of the fields' contents and also be as short as possible. For example, instead of PART NUMBER and QUANTITY ON HAND you could use PNUM and QOH.

After you have made these decisions, creating the database table is quite simple.

To create a new database table:

1. Select a worksheet region that has enough empty space to hold the table without interfering with other worksheet data. It's a good idea to devote an entire worksheet to your database table.

2. Enter the field names in the first row of the database table.

3. Enter the data for the first record in the second row of the table. It's important that the first record be in the row directly below the field names; do not use any sort of separators.

4. Enter data for additional records in the third and subsequent rows.

5. If desired, change formatting, label alignment, and column width to best display the data.

Name That Range It's a good idea to assign a name to the database table range. Be sure that the range includes all rows and columns in the table. See Lesson 6 for more information on assigning range names.

No Blank Rows! A database table cannot contain any blank rows. Individual records may contain one or more blank fields, as long as at least one field in the record contains data.

To add data to an existing database table, simply move to the first blank row and begin entering the new data.

Data contained in a database table differs from other worksheet data only in that it is organized into a record/field structure. Otherwise it is no different from any other worksheet data. You can graph it, print it, edit it, copy it to other worksheets, use it in calculations, and so on. 1-2-3 for Windows also has some special capabilities designed specifically for use with database tables. The next two lessons deal with the most important of these capabilities.

In this lesson, you learned the fundamentals of creating a 1-2-3 for Windows database. The next lesson shows you how to sort the data in a database table.

Sorting a Database

In this lesson, you'll learn how to sort a database table.

Sorting a Database

When working with a database table, one common task you'll need to perform is to sort your database records into a particular order. For example, you could sort a mailing list database into ZIP code order before printing mailing labels, or sort a customer database by amount of sale to find your best customers. 1-2-3 for Windows can sort a database table based on the contents of one or more fields. A field that is used to determine sort order is called a *sort key*.

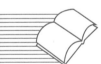

Sort Key A database field whose contents are used to determine the sort order.

You always use at least one sort key to order the records when sorting a database. Records in the database table are sorted according to the data in the sort key field. If the sort key is a value field, records are sorted into numerical order. If the sort key is a label field, the following order is used:

- Blank cells

- Labels beginning with a space

- Labels beginning with a number

- Labels beginning with a letter, in alphabetical order (lowercase letters have precedence over uppercase letters)

- Labels beginning with other characters

Besides the primary sort key field, you have the option of specifying one or more additional sort keys, which will be used to order the records when there is a tie in the first sort key field. The sort order can be either ascending or descending. When you select ascending sort order, labels are sorted alphabetically A-Z, and numbers are sorted smallest to largest. When you select descending order, labels are sorted Z-A, and numbers are sorted largest to smallest.

To sort a database table:

1. Highlight the worksheet range that includes all of the database table records but not the database table field names.

2. Select **R**ange **S**ort to display the Sort dialog box (see Figure 21.1).

3. In the **S**ort By text box, enter the address of any cell in the column that contains the field you want the records sorted by.

Figure 21.1 You specify sort keys in the Sort dialog box.

4. To add more sort keys, click on the Add Key button and repeat step 3 to specify the address of a cell in the secondary sort key field.

5. To clear all sort keys, click on Reset.

6. Click OK to perform the sort.

Field Names in the Sort Range If you mistakenly include the database table's field names in the sort range, they will be sorted like any other record. To recover, use the Edit Undo command.

When a database table is sorted, the sorted records are placed in the same worksheet range as the original table. No changes are made to data in the database; only the position of records in the table is changed.

Saving the Original Order If you want to retain the original database record order, as well as the new sorted order, first copy the database table to a new worksheet location and then sort the copy.

In this lesson, you learned how to sort the records in a database. The next lesson shows you how to find specific information in a database.

Lesson 22

Searching a Database

In this lesson, you'll learn how to find information in your database.

Searching for Information

When you have created a database, you'll often need to locate specific records. For example:

- In a mailing list database, find all addresses in New York.

- In a parts inventory database, find all parts with fewer than 5 on hand.

A search for specific information in a database is called a *query*. A query finds the records that meet one or more criteria. In the above examples, STATE = NY is a criterion, as is Quantity On Hand less than 5. To perform a query, you must specify exactly the criteria you are interested in.

Query To search for specific information in a database.

Criteria Basics

To search a database, you must indicate your criteria, which specifies exactly what information you are looking for. When setting up criteria, there are a number of operators, or symbols, that you can use. Each operator tells 1-2-3 how to compare data in the database table with your criteria. The operator symbols are listed here in Table 22.1.

Table 22.1   1-2-3 operator symbols.

Symbol	Meaning
=	equal to
<>	not equal to
>	greater than
<	less than
<=	less than or equal to
>=	greater than or equal to

When applied to values, these operators have their usual meanings. For example, the symbol < tells 1-2-3 to accept only those records where the value in the field is less than the criterion you specified. When applied to labels, the operators refer to alphabetical order. Thus, when applied to a label field, the symbol < tells 1-2-3 to accept only those records where the data in the field is alphabetically "before" the criterion.

If you use more than one criterion in a query, you must tell 1-2-3 how to combine the various criteria. For example, if you have specified two criteria, you must specify whether a record in the database table must meet both criteria to be considered a "match," or if meeting only one of the criteria is sufficient. Pairs of criteria can be combined with either the AND connector or the OR connector:

- If two criteria are connected with AND, a record is considered a match only if it meets both criteria.

- If two criteria are connected with OR, a record is considered a match if it meets only one, or both, of the criteria.

Performing a Query

When you perform a query, you must provide 1-2-3 with certain information:

- What is the range of the database table to search?

- What are the criteria to be met?

- Where should the results be placed?

Once you have provided this information, 1-2-3 looks at each record in the database table to see if it meets the criteria that you specified. Every record that meets the criteria is copied to the output location. For example, Figure 22.1 shows the result of a query on the database table in the range A1..D8. The criteria was "Quantity on Hand less than 10." You can see that the four records that meet this criteria have been copied to the range A12..D16.

To perform a query on a database table:

1. Highlight the entire database table, including the field names in the first row.

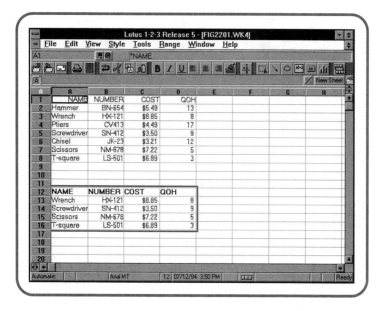

Figure 22.1   The result of a query on a database table.

2. Select **T**ools Data**b**ase **N**ew Query to display the New Query Assistant dialog box (see Figure 22.2).

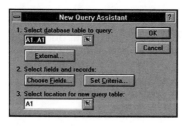

Figure 22.2   The New Query dialog box.

3. Select Set Criteria to display the Set Criteria dialog box shown in Figure 22.3.

Figure 22.3   The Set Criteria dialog box.

4. If necessary, select **C**lear to delete any exiting criteria in the Criteria list.

5. Select a database field from the **F**ield drop-down box.

6. Select a comparison operator from the O**p**erator drop-down box.

7. Enter the criterion in the **V**alue box or drop down the box to select from a list of all values present in the specified field in the database.

8. To enter an additional criteria, click the **A**nd or the **O**r button to connect the criteria. Then repeat steps 5 through 7 to specify the second criterion.

9. Select OK to return to the New Query Assistant dialog box.

10. In the Select location for new **q**uery table box, enter the address where you want the results of the query placed.

11. Select OK. 1-2-3 performs the query and copies the matching records, if any, to the specified location.

Finding Records

You can find records in a database table that meet certain criteria. Rather than copying the matching records to a different part of the worksheet, 1-2-3 will highlight the matching records in the database table. You can then examine the records, modify them, and so on. To find records:

1. Highlight the entire database table, including the field names in the first row.

2. Select Tools Database Find Records to display the Find Records dialog box (see Figure 22.4).

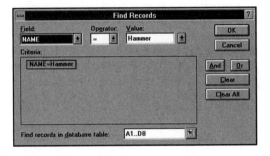

Figure 22.4 The Find Records dialog box.

3. In the dialog box, specify your criteria as described earlier in this lesson.

4. Click OK. 1-2-3 highlights all matching records in the database table.

You can then work with the highlighted records in the following ways:

- To go to the next matching record, press Ctrl+Enter.

- To go to the previous matching record, press Ctrl+Shift+Enter.

- To go to the next field in the current record, press Enter.

- To go to the previous field in the current record, press Shift+Enter.

- To edit the current cell, press F2, make the desired changes, and then press Enter.

- To deselect the highlighted records, press Esc or click in any cell.

This is the final lesson in the *10 Minute Guide to 1-2-3 for Windows*. You now should know enough about the program to start using it for real-world tasks.

Appendix A
Microsoft Windows Primer

Microsoft Windows is an interface program that makes your computer easier to use by allowing you to select menu items and pictures rather than type commands. Before you can take advantage of it, however, you must learn some Windows basics.

Starting Microsoft Windows

To start Windows, do the following:

1. At the DOS prompt, type `win`.

2. Press Enter.

The Windows title screen appears for a few moments, and then you see a screen like the one in Figure A.1.

What If It Didn't Work? You may have to change to the Windows directory before starting Windows; to do so, type `CD \WINDOWS` and press Enter.

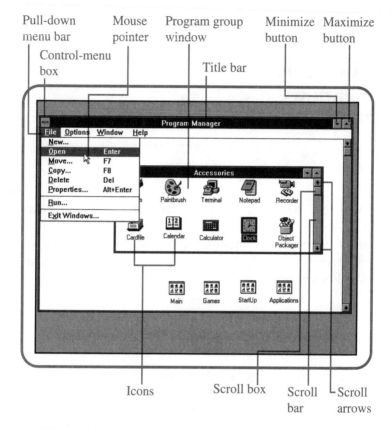

Pull-down
menu bar

Mouse
pointer

Program group
window

Minimize
button

Maximize
button

Control-menu
box

Title bar

Icons   Scroll box   Scroll   Scroll
                               bar   arrows

Figure A.1   The Windows Program Manager.

Parts of a Windows Screen

As shown in Figure A.1, the Windows screen contains several unique elements that you won't see in DOS. Here's a brief summary.

- *Title bar*   Shows the name of the window or program.

- *Program group windows*   Contain program icons which allow you to run programs.

- *Icons*   Graphic representations of programs. To run a program, you select its icon.

- *Minimize and Maximize buttons*   Alter a window's size. The Minimize button shrinks the window to the size of an icon. The Maximize button expands the window to fill the screen. When maximized, a window contains a double-arrow *Restore* button, which returns the window to its original size.

- *Control-menu box*   When selected, pulls down a menu that offers size and location controls for the window.

- *Pull-down menu bar*   Contains a list of the pull-down menus available in the program.

- *Mouse pointer*   If you are using a mouse, the mouse pointer (usually an arrow) appears on-screen. It can be controlled by moving the mouse (discussed later in this appendix).

- *Scroll bars*   If a window contains more information than can be displayed in the window, a scroll bar appears. *Scroll arrows* on each end of the scroll bar allow you to scroll slowly. The *scroll box* allows you to scroll more quickly.

Using a Mouse

To work most efficiently in Windows, you should use a mouse. You can press mouse buttons and move the mouse in various ways to change the way it acts:

Point means to move the mouse pointer onto the specified item by moving the mouse. The tip of the mouse pointer must be touching the item.

149

Click on an item means to move the pointer onto the specified item and press the mouse button once. Unless specified otherwise, use the left mouse button.

Double-click on an item means to move the pointer onto the specified item and press and release the mouse button twice quickly.

Drag means to move the mouse pointer onto the specified item, hold down the mouse button, and move the mouse while holding down the button.

Starting a Program

To start a program, simply select its icon. If its icon is contained in a program group window that's not currently open, open the window first. Follow these steps:

1. If necessary, open the program group window that contains the program you want to run. To open a program group window, double-click on its icon.

2. Double-click on the icon for the program you want to run.

Using Menus

The pull-down menu bar (see Figure A.2) contains various menus from which you can select commands. Each Windows program that you run has a set of pull-down menus; Windows itself has a set too.

To open a menu, click on its name on the menu bar. Once a menu is open, you can select a command from it by clicking on the desired command.

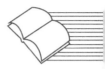

Accelerator Keys Notice that in Figure A.2, some commands are followed by key names such as Enter (for the **O**pen command) or F8 (for the **C**opy command). These are called *accelerator keys*. You can use these keys to perform the command without even opening the menu.

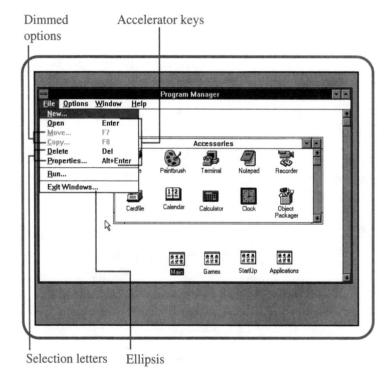

Figure A.2 A menu lists various commands you can perform.

Usually, when you select a command, the command is performed immediately. However:

• If the command name is gray (rather than black), the command is unavailable at the moment and you cannot choose it.

• If the command name is followed by an arrow, selecting the command will cause another menu to appear, from which you select another command.

• If the command name is followed by an ellipsis (three dots), selecting it will cause a dialog box to appear. You'll learn about dialog boxes in the next section.

Navigating Dialog Boxes

A dialog box is Windows' way of requesting additional information. For example, if you choose **P**rint from the **F**ile menu in the Write application, you'll see the dialog box shown in Figure A.3.

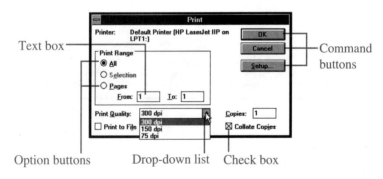

Figure A.3 A typical dialog box.

Each dialog box contains one or more of the following elements:

- *List boxes* display available choices. To activate a list, click inside the list box. If the entire list is not visible, use the scroll bar to view the items in the list. To select an item from the list, click on it.

- *Drop-down lists* are similar to list boxes, but only one item in the list is shown. To see the rest of the items, click on the down arrow to the right of the list box. To select an item from the list, click on it.

- *Text boxes* allow you to type an entry. To activate a text box, click inside it. To edit an existing entry, use the arrow keys to move the cursor and the Del or Backspace keys to delete existing characters. Then type your correction.

- *Check boxes* allow you to select one or more items in a group of options. For example, if you are styling text, you may select Bold and Italic to have the text appear in both bold and italic type. Click on a check box to activate it.

- *Option buttons* are like check boxes, but you can select only one option button in a group. Selecting one button unselects any option that is already selected. Click on an option button to activate it.

- *Command buttons* execute (or cancel) the command once you have made your selections in the dialog box. To press a command button, click on it.

Switching Between Windows

Many times you will have more than one window open at once. Some open windows may be program group windows, while others may be actual programs that are running. To switch among them, you can:

- Pull down the Window menu and choose the window you want to view.

or

- If a portion of the desired window is visible, click on it.

Controlling and Resizing a Window

As you saw earlier in this appendix, you can minimize, maximize, and restore windows on-screen. But you can also move them and change their size.

- To move a window, drag its title bar to a different location. (Remember, "drag" means to hold down the left mouse button while you move the mouse.)

- To resize a window, position the mouse pointer on the border of the window until you see a double-headed arrow; then drag the window border to the desired size.

Copying Your Program Diskettes with File Manager

Before you install any new software, you should make a copy of the original diskettes as a safety precaution. Windows' File Manager makes this process easy.

First, start File Manager by double-clicking on the File Manager icon in the Main program group. Then, for each disk you need to copy, follow these steps:

1. Locate a blank disk of the same type as the original disk, and label it to match the original. Make sure the disk you select does not contain any data that you want to keep.

2. Place the original disk in your diskette drive (A or B).

3. Open the Disk menu and select Copy Disk. The Copy Disk dialog box appears.

4. From the Source In list box, select the drive used in step 2.

5. Select the same drive from the Destination In list box. (Don't worry; File Manager will tell you to switch disks at the appropriate time.)

6. Select OK. The Confirm Copy Disk dialog box appears.

7. Select Yes to continue.

8. When instructed to insert the Source diskette, choose OK, since you already did this in step 2. The Copying Disk box appears, and the copy process begins.

9. When instructed to insert the target disk, remove the original disk from the drive and insert the blank disk. Then choose OK to continue. The Copying Disk box disappears when the process is complete.

Appendix B

Table of Functions

Following are the most commonly used @functions.

Statistical Functions

@function	Value or action	Example
@COUNT	The number of nonblank cells in a range.	@COUNT(A1..A100) Returns the number of nonblank cells in the range A1..A100.
@MAX	The maximum value in a range.	@MAX(SALES) Returns the largest value in any cell in the named range SALES.
@MIN	The minimum value in a range.	@MIN(SALES) Returns the smallest value in any cell in the named range SALES.
@AVG	The arithmetic average of values in a range.	@AVG(SALES) Returns the average of all values in the named range SALES.

@function	Value or action	Example
@STD	The standard deviation of values in a range.	@STD(B1..B20) Returns the standard deviation of the values in the range B1..B20.
@SUM	The sum of values in a range.	@SUM(B1..B20) Returns the sum of all values in the range B1..B20.

Mathematical and Trigonometric Functions

@function	Value or action	Example
@ABS	The absolute (positive) value of a value.	@ABS(A1) Returns the value in cell A1 converted to a positive value.
@LN	The natural logarithm of a value.	@LN(B20) Returns the natural logarithm of the value in cell B20.
@SQRT	The square root of a value.	@SQRT(D6) The square root of the value in cell D6.
@SIN	The sine of an angle.	@SIN(A5) The sine of the angle in cell A5.
@RAND	A random number.	@RAND Returns a random number between 0 and 1.
@ROUND	Rounds a value to a specified number of decimal places.	@ROUND(1.45612,2) Returns the value 1.45612 to 2 decimal places (i.e., 1.46).

Financial Functions

@function	Value or action	Example
@PMT	The periodic payment on a loan with given amount, interest rate, and term.	@PMT(2000,.1/12, 36) Returns the monthly payment on a 36 month loan at 10% annual interest.
@IRR	The internal rate of return for a series of cash flows.	@IRR(0.1,A1..A50) Returns the internal rate of return for the cash flow values in the range A1..A50, with an initial guess of 10%.
@FV	The future value of a series of equal payments.	@FV(100,.1/12, 120) Returns the total amount you will have if you invest $100 per month for 10 years (120 months) in an account that pays 10% annual interest.

Logical Functions

@function	Value or action	Example
@ISSTRING	Determines if a worksheet cell contains a label.	@ISSTRING(A1) Returns 1 (true) if cell A1 contains a label, 0 (false) if not.
@IF	Evaluates a condition and returns one value if it is true, another if it is false.	@IF(A1>A2,1,0) Returns 1 if the value in cell A1 is greater than the value in cell A2; returns 0 otherwise.

Date and Time Functions

@function	Value or action	Example
@TIME	The time serial number for a specified time.	@TIME(6,30,0) Returns the time serial number corresponding to 6:30AM.
@TODAY	The date serial number corresponding to today's date.	@TODAY Returns the date serial number corresponding to the date set on the computer's system clock.
@DATE	The date serial number for a given date.	@DATE(93,12,25) Returns the date serial number for December 25, 1993.
@YEAR	The year of a date serial number.	@YEAR(A1) Returns the year of the date serial number in cell A1.

159

Index

Symbols

$ (dollar sign), 62
% (percent sign), 71
' (left aligned prefix), 27
" (right aligned prefix), 28
* (asterisks), 74
* (multiplication operator), 60
+ (addition operator), 60
- (subtraction operator), 60
/ (division operator), 60
< (less than operator), 141
<= (less than or equal to operator), 141
<> (not equal to operator), 141
= (equal to operator), 141
> (greater than operator), 141
>= (greater than or equal to operator), 141
^ (centered prefixes), 28
^ (exponentiation operator), 60
100% axis scale, 121
3-D ranges, *see* three-dimensional ranges
3D charts, 104-105

A

absolute addresses, 61-62
accelerator keys, 7, 151
addition operator (+), 60

addresses
 cells, 17, 61-62
 ranges, 42
alignment, 74-77
Alignment command, 75
Alignment dialog box, 75
arcs, 125-126
area charts, 3D, 104-105
arguments, @functions, 65
arrow keys, 8
arrowheads, 7, 129
arrows, 125-126
attributes, fonts, 87-88
Automatic format numbers, 72
Axis command, 119
axes, 105, 119-123
axis unit titles, 119, 122-123
Axis X-Axis command, 121
Axis Y-Axis command, 121

B

bar charts, 3D, 104-105
blank fields (database tables), 134
blank rows (database tables), 134
borders, 88-90

C

calculations, 60, 63-64
 see also numeric calculations
calendar @functions, 63
cancelling, 9, 26, 42

captions, text blocks, 126
cascade menus, 6-9
cell pointer, moving, 3, 17, 20, 24
cell references, *see* addresses
cells
    addresses, 17, 57-65
    contents, deleting, 48
    fonts, 79
    formats, 69
    information, @functions, 64
characters, 27-29
    see also labels
charts, 102-118
Charts command, 106
check boxes, 11, 154
circles, 126
Clear command, 49
Clear Split command, 23
clearing sort keys, 138
clicking mouse, 150
Clipboard, 46-48
Close command, 37
closing
    files, 37
    Print Preview window, 96
    worksheets, 37
color
    fonts, selecting, 87
    graphics, selecting, 128-129
Column Width command, 81
columns, 52-56, 132
    data series, 108-109
    fonts, default, 79
    inserting, 52-54
    labels, displaying, 78
    ranges, selecting, 42
    row height, 83
    width, 74, 78-82
combining worksheets, 37
Comma format, numbers, 70
command buttons, 11, 154
commands, 4-9
    dialog boxes, 7-11, 152
    ranges, selecting, 40
    selecting, 7-9, 151
    undoing, 50

commas, numbers, 70
compressing printing, 98
converting to serial numbers, 30
Confirm box, data entry, 26
contents box, 3
    data entry, 26
    labels, editing, 31
control-menu box, screen, 149
Copy command, 48, 62
copying
    data, 46-48
    formulas, 62
    graphics, 128
    program diskettes (Windows),
        155-156
Currency format, 70
current cell, 17, 26
Cut command, 48, 111

D

data types, 25-27, 133
data series (charts), 102, 105,
    108-109
database @functions, 63
Database Find Records command,
    145
Database New Query command,
    143
databases, 31, 131-142, 145-146
dates, 29-30, 63, 72, 99, 161-162
debugging formulas, 71
decimal places, 70, 72, 74
default styles, 49
defining current selections, 39-45
Delete command, 55
deleting, 49
    attributes, fonts, 88
    cell contents, 48
    charts, 111
    columns, 54-56
    data, 30-32, 48-49
    frames, 89
    graphics, 128
    rows, 54-56

dialog boxes, 7-11, 153-154
directories, selecting, 34, 36
disks, saving to, 33-35
displaying
    dates, 72
    files, 35-37
    results, formulas, 59
    time, 72
    worksheets, 35-37
division operator (/), 60
double-clicking mouse, 150
dragging mouse, 150
Draw command, 125
Draw Text command, 127
drives, selecting, 34-36
drop-down boxes, 10
drop-down lists, 153

E

editing
    data, insertion point, 31
    data entry, 30-32
    formulas, 60
ellipses, 7, 39, 126
End key, moving cell pointer, 20
engineering @functions, 64
entering
    @functions, selector, 67
    dates, 29-30
    formulas, 58-60
    time, 29-30
    titles, 119
    values, 27
entries, editing, 27
equal to operator (=), 141
erasing, *see* deleting
errors, formulas, 59
executing queries, 142-144
exiting 1-2-3 for Windows, 4
expanding print range, 98
exponentiation operator (^), 60
exponents, specifying, 122

F

fields, 132-138
file names, 34, 99
files, 20-21, 33-37
financial @functions, 64, 159
Font & Attributes commands,
    86-87
fonts, 79, 85-88
footers, 99
footnotes, charts, 113-118
formats, 69-77, 90-92
formulas, 57-64, 71
frames, 88-100
@functions, 63-68, 158-162

G

graphics, 124-130
grayed menu items, 7
greater than operator (>), 141
greater than or equal to operator
    (>=), 141
grids, printing, 100

H

handles (graphics), 128
headers, 99
Headings command, 114-115
Help, 35, 64
Hidden format, numbers, 71
hiding data, 71
HLCO chart, 104
horizontal alignment, modifying,
    74-76

I

icon screen, 149
information @functions, 64
information boxes, 10
Insert command, 21, 52-54
insertion points, 31

J-K-L

labels, 25-27
    @functions, 64
    alignment, default, 74, 77
    assigning, 117
    displaying, 27
    editing in contents box, 31
    entering, 27-29
    fields, 136
    legends, 108-109
    length, 29
    operators, 141
    prefixes, 27-29
    sorting, 137
landscape orientation, 98
Legend command, 116
legends, 108-109, 115-118
less than operator (<), 141
less than or equal to operator (<=), 141
line charts, 3D, 104-105
lines, 125-129
Lines & Color command, 89, 129
list boxes, 10, 153
listing files, 36
logarithmic axis scales, 121
logical @functions, 64, 159-160
lookup @functions, 64
Lotus Applications window, 1-2

M

margins, 97
mathematical @functions, 64, 158
mathematical operators, 60-61
maximize buttons, screen, 149
memory, RAM (random access memory), 33
menu bar, 2, 5
menu pointer, 7-8
menus, 5-8, 151-152
minimize buttons, screen, 149
mixed chart, 104
mode indicator, data types, 25

mouse, 149-150
moving
    charts, 110-111
    data to clipboard, 48
    footnotes, charts, 117-118
    graphics, 128
    insertion point, 31
    legends, charts, 117-118
    titles, charts, 117-118
    windows, 154-156
multi-cell selections, *see* ranges
multiplication operator (*), 60

N

Name command, 44-45
Named Style command, 90-91
named styles, 90-92
names
    assigning, 34
    defaults, 33
    fields, databases, 132, 138
    formats, displaying, 72
    @functions, 65
    ranges, database tables, 44-45, 134
navigating records, 146
New command, 37
not equal to operator (<>), 141
notes, text blocks, 126
Number Format command, 69, 73
numbers, 69-74
    decimal places, displaying, 70
    displaying, 70-74
    formats, 69-73
    negative, displaying, 70
    rounding, 70
    see also values
numeric calculations, formulas, 60
    see also calculations

O

objects, printing, 100
Open command, 35

opening
  files, 35-37
  pull-down menus, 151
  worksheets, 35-37
operating systems, 64
operators, 60-61, 141
option buttons, 11, 154

P

page numbers, 99
page setup, changing, 96-101
Page Setup command, 96
Paste command, 48, 111
Percent format, numbers, 71
perspective view, 22
pie charts, 3D, 104-105
plotting data series, 102, 105
POINT mode, @functions, 66
pointers, 8, 17
portrait orientation, 98
precedence, operators, 61
prefixes, 27-29
Preview command, 95
previewing fonts, 87
Print command, 94, 112
Print Preview, 95-96
printing, 93-100
program group windows, 148
Program Manager window, 1
pull-down menus, 4-9, 149-152

Q-R

queries, databases, 140-144
question mark icon, 35
quick menu, 6-7
  commands, selecting, 9
  displaying, 48, 56

radar chart, 104
range information, @functions, 64
ranges, 39-45
  formats, changing, 73-74
  printing, 98
  styles, assigning, 91

records, databases, 131, 145-146
recovering data, 50
rectangles, 126
relative addresses, 61-62
replacing
  data entry, 30-32
  existing entries, 26
resizing floating SmartIcon
    window, 13
restoring
  default, axis scales, 122
  original data, 31
  row height, 84
rounded rectangles, 126
Row Height command, 84
rows, 132
  data series, 108
  deleting, 54-56
  height, 82-84
  inserting, 52-54
  selecting, 56

S

Save command, 33
saving, 33-35, 100, 111, 138
scaling printouts, 97-98
scatter chart, *see* XY chart
screen, 1-4, 148-149
scroll bars, 149
scrolling, 18-20
searching, criteria, 140-142
selecting
  3D ranges, 43-44
  arrowhead positions, lines, 129
  charts, 109-110
  color, 87, 129
  columns, 56
  data series for charts, 105
  graphics, 128
  names, fonts, 87
  ranges, 40-42
  styles, lines, 129
selection indicator, 2
serial numbers, 29, 72

Set View Preferences command, 14
sizing
    charts, 110-111
    fonts, 85
    graphics, 128
    ranges, 39
    windows, 154-156
SmartIcons, 3, 12-13
SmartIcons command, 14
sort order, saving, 138
Sort command, 137
sort keys, 136-138
sorting, 136-139
special @functions, 161
Split command, 23
squares, 126
standard axis scale, 121
starting
    1-2-3 for Windows, 1-2
    programs, 151
    Windows, 147-148
statistical @functions, 64, 157-158
storing time/date, 29-30
string @functions, 160
styles, 48-49, 129
subtitles, charts, 113-115
subtraction operator (-), 60
syntax, formulas, 58

T

tables, databases, 132-135
text
    blocks, 126-127
    formulas, displaying, 71
    rotating, 76
    see also labels
text @functions, 64
text boxes, 10, 153
Text format, 60, 71
three-dimensional ranges, 42-44
time, 29-30, 63, 72, 99
title bar, screen, 2, 6, 148
titles, 109, 113-121
transparent graphics, 130

trigonometric @functions, 158
Type command, 110

U-V

underlined letters (commands), 7
Undo command, 49-51
unit title, *see* axis unit titles
updating cell references, 54
User Setup command, 49

value fields, 136
values, 25-27
    formulas, 57
    operators, 141
    rounding, 70
vertical scroll bar, list boxes, 10

W

Windows, screen, 147-149
windows, 95, 154-156
Worksheet Defaults command, 76
worksheets, 16-17
    closing, 37
    combining, 37
    displaying, 35-37
    inserting into files, 20-21
    moving between, 22
    multiple, viewing, 22-24
    naming, 17
    navigating, 18-22
    opening, 35-37
    perspective view, 22
    saving, 33-35
    selecting, 42
    window, 3
wrapping text, labels, 76

X-Y-Z

X-axis title, 119-121
XY chart, 104

Y-axis title, 119-121